"If you're feeling easily triggered, guilty, and overwhelmed by parenting, you're not alone—and there's nothing wrong with you. In *Love Your Kids Without Losing Yourself,* Dr. Morgan Cutlip explains why so many of us feel this way and offers a practical five-step method to reduce mom burnout. There's no laundry list of self-care strategies here; instead, you will leave this book feeling equipped and empowered to take care of yourself and manage the day-to-day of motherhood."

—DR. BECKY KENNEDY, CLINICAL PSYCHOLOGIST, FOUNDER AND CEO OF GOOD INSIDE, AND #1 *NEW YORK TIMES* BESTSELLING AUTHOR

"Dr. Morgan unpacks a topic every mom needs to hear about (including me)! Motherhood can be so challenging—add in everything else going on in our lives, and we can feel like we're losing. But Dr. Morgan does an incredible job encouraging us moms with truth and practical ways to love our kids and ourselves more. I'm so thankful moms everywhere will hear this message!"

—RACHEL CRUZE, *NEW YORK TIMES* BESTSELLING AUTHOR AND PERSONAL FINANCE EXPERT

"A must read for busy moms who have been on the back burner for way too long. Dr. Morgan gives moms a practical plan to feel whole in motherhood. *Love Your Kids Without Losing Yourself* offers solutions to the most relevant issues moms face but offers these tools in a relatable and digestible way. If you feel overwhelmed or lost in motherhood, you need this book."

—DR. SHEFALI TSABARY, *NEW YORK TIMES* BESTSELLING AUTHOR AND CLINICAL PSYCHOLOGIST

"Get this book into the hands of every mom, stat! Dr. Morgan expertly recognizes the identity struggle modern moms suffer with and provides encouragement and practical tools to help. You will find yourself nodding along with, underlining in, highlighting in, and loaning this book to each of your fellow mom friends."

—MANDY ARIOTO, PRESIDENT AND CEO OF MOPS INTERNATIONAL

"Want to rid yourself of mom-guilt for good? Dr. Morgan Cutlip shows you how. You'll laugh out loud as you read *Love Your Kids Without Losing Yourself*. You'll also discover a practical and proven plan for becoming the mom you want to be. We're not exaggerating when we say that reading this book just may be the most important thing you do all year for your kids, as well as for yourself."

—DRS. LES AND LESLIE PARROTT, #1 *NEW YORK TIMES* BESTSELLING AUTHORS OF *SAVING YOUR MARRIAGE BEFORE IT STARTS*

"I will admit, I usually expect books like this to just add to the overwhelm and pile more on a mom's plate that is already incredibly full. But *Love Your Kids Without Losing Yourself* brings an entirely new perspective to the mom-burnout conversation. Dr. Morgan reminds moms that they require the same care that they provide to all their other relationships and offers five important steps to help moms care for themselves in deep and meaningful ways without piling more on. Every mom needs this book."

—ASHLEY LEMIEUX, MENTAL WELLNESS AND GRIEF EXPERT AND BESTSELLING AUTHOR OF *I AM HERE*

"As a social researcher who is a frazzled mom and who talks to a lot of frazzled moms, I can tell you that this book is the one we've all been waiting for! Dr. Morgan shares the eye-opening truth that thriving in motherhood is not about somehow finding the perfect balance. It's about how to make slight changes in our day-to-day lives that make a real difference in how we love ourselves and our kids well. This is going to give every mom less stress and more peace."

—SHAUNTI FELDHAHN, BESTSELLING AUTHOR OF *FOR WOMEN ONLY* AND *FIND REST*

# love
# your kids
## *without*
# losing
# yourself

# love
# your kids
## *without*
# losing
# yourself

**5 STEPS TO BANISH GUILT AND BEAT BURNOUT
WHEN YOU ALREADY HAVE TOO MUCH TO DO**

## DR. MORGAN CUTLIP

NELSON
BOOKS

An Imprint of Thomas Nelson

The Relationship Attachment Model is used with permission from John Van Epp, first developed in 1992.

Published in Nashville, Tennessee, by Nelson Books, an imprint of Thomas Nelson. Nelson Books and Thomas Nelson are registered trademarks of HarperCollins Christian Publishing, Inc.

The author is represented by Alive Literary Agency, www.aliveliterary.com.

Thomas Nelson titles may be purchased in bulk for educational, business, fundraising, or sales promotional use. For information, please email SpecialMarkets@ThomasNelson.com.

The information in this book has been carefully researched by the author and is intended to be a source of information only. Readers are urged to consult with their physicians or other professional advisors to address specific medical or other issues. The author and the publisher assume no responsibility for any injuries suffered or damages incurred during or as a result of the use or application of the information contained herein.

Names and identifying characteristics of some individuals have been changed to preserve their privacy.

ISBN 978-1-4002-3966-5 (TP)

### Library of Congress Cataloging-in-Publication Data

Names: Cutlip, Morgan, 1982- author.
Title: Love your kids without losing yourself : 5 steps to banish guild and beat burnout when you already have too much to do / Dr. Morgan Cutlip.
Description: Nashville, Tennessee : Nelson Books, [2023] | Summary: "Relationship expert and counselor Dr. Morgan Cutlip equips mothers with five simple steps for combating the chaos of motherhood, defeating feelings of guilt and inadequacy, and deeply loving their kids without neglecting or losing themselves"-- Provided by publisher.
Identifiers: LCCN 2023013474 (print) | LCCN 2023013475 (ebook) | ISBN 9781400239627 (hardcover) | ISBN 9781400239641 (ebook)
Subjects: LCSH: Motherhood. | Parenting. | Parent and child. | Guilt.
Classification: LCC HQ759 .C987 2023 (print) | LCC HQ759 (ebook) | DDC 306.874/3--dc23/eng/20230418
LC record available at https://lccn.loc.gov/2023013474
LC ebook record available at https://lccn.loc.gov/2023013475

*Printed in the United States of America*

24 25 26 27 28 LBC 5 4 3 2 1

*To Effie and Roy. My life is infinitely better
because I get to be your mom.*

# CONTENTS

# CONTENTS

# BALANCE IS BALONEY

This book is for you if:

- You spin through your day at warp speed but never feel like you're enough or that you get enough done.
- You don't recognize yourself anymore and feel just generally uninspired.
- You don't feel like a whole person in your family. It's almost like the boundaries between you and your family have blurred and you're unsure where they end and you begin.
- You're doing all the things for your family and kids but you're still haunted by guilt.
- You're weary and exhausted and you're sick of the typical "take a walk" advice.
- Whenever you have a moment to yourself, you have no idea how to spend it in a way that actually offers true rest and reprieve from your busy pace.
- You're desperate for a new perspective on "self-care" for moms. You know the problem but you've yet to find a solution that actually makes a meaningful difference.
- You're hesitant to make changes and upset the balance in

your family but you know that you can't keep going on as
you are now.

I just want to acknowledge for a moment something I believe is
almost a universal desire of moms and that is that we want to be
good moms, but we also want to *feel good in motherhood.*

My guess is that you've got the good mom part down (more on
that to come) but the feeling good part has been more difficult to
come by.

In the pages that follow you will be offered a new approach
to motherhood that you haven't seen anywhere else. I feel confi-
dent that you will benefit from what's inside this book because I
struggled with each point in that bulleted list, and when I imple-
mented the tools and system I am going to share with you, I found
so much more peace and joy in motherhood. The content of this
book is consistent with research but is explained in a simple, practical way and I can assure you that you will leave each chapter with
actionable skills you can use right away.

## MY WHY

I have a confession.

I thought I would be one of the best moms that ever lived. I realize that's ridiculous, so maybe top 100 or so, since the world is a
pretty big place. Allow me to justify my expectation. I have a degree
in human development and family science. I'm not sure what that
actually did for me, but I thought it would, at least, offer some
assurance I was prepared for motherhood. I also have a doctorate
in psychology—that has to do something for my mothering skills,
right? My father also has his doctorate in psychology, and I grew
up in a family that had "family meetings" and did *those* types of
things. I had an excellent mother who provided a top-notch example

of what a "good mom" looks like. I mean, I had all the makings of a top 100 mom.

I went into motherhood knowing how I wanted to discipline our kids. I imagined doing time-outs; before you slam this book shut, I realize those are out of fashion to many now. But it's what I grew up with, and therefore it's what I figured I'd do. I imagined our three-year-old sitting in time-out thoughtfully examining her poor choices and me bending down to meet her at eye level and putting all my psychological skill set to use, analyzing her behavior with her and talking about her plan for making better choices in the future. We'd hug and skip off into the sunset holding hands. Easy peasy.

The thing is, I made one massive oversight. I never factored in the type of kid we would have. I have a stinkin' degree in human development and family science and I didn't factor in temperament.

Our daughter, Effie, was born with preferences. She came out having strong opinions and gave me a total run for my money. She's a ball of fire and incredible, but I really wasn't prepared for her at all.

When Effie was born, my husband, Chad, and I were living in Florida. We had just moved there from the DC area to be close to my parents. If you don't know this, when you're from the East Coast and you get close to retirement, you move to Florida. That's what my parents did and we realized we didn't want to be without family and support when we had kids, so we followed them there. When we moved into our house in Florida, I was nine months pregnant. Around the time Effie was two months old, Chad was offered a promotion that required relocating to California. He had turned several down already, so this one came as a sort of promotion /ultimatum situation.

This was a painful decision, but he took the job and we decided that he would go to California and I would stay in Florida near my family until we found a new home. Looking back, I think I would have made the same decision, because he was busy and overwhelmed adjusting to his new role and I needed the support. But it was a really difficult time.

We spent the next eight months apart, seeing each other every other weekend or so. If you're already a mom, you know all that happens in those eight months: the dreaded four-month sleep regression and introducing solids. I breastfed, so you can imagine the shock and stink when her poop changed. Oh my! I spent so many nights feeding Effie in the darkness of her room feeling deep loneliness and despair, wondering, *Will I ever sleep again?* I read all the sleep blogs in existence at the time; I figured there had to be a way of cracking this code. Looking back, her sleep was totally normal. I wish I had saved my sanity and just accepted that exhaustion was a normal part of early parenthood.

As Effie got older, her temperament didn't really change, it just got bigger and louder. And by the time I finally met up with Chad in California, I had become so accustomed to taking care of her "my way" that I didn't make much space for him to step in. And his lack of experience over those early months bred such a feeling of insecurity in managing our very opinionated baby that he didn't do a great job of inserting himself either.

I was exhausted. I didn't recognize myself anymore. And I was burned-out, becoming very bitter, and buried by my overwhelm in early motherhood.

I thought I would be really good at being a mom. Yet I was constantly confronted with feelings of falling short. I felt guilty asking for any time for myself, caught off guard by how much freedom I had lost, confused about how to manage Effie's personality, and disconnected from who I knew myself to be. I was lost in motherhood and it felt heavy.

This is what happens to so many of us: we lose ourselves in our children, feel overwhelmed and stifled by motherhood, and then come up for air just to be filled with guilt and shame. We either swing like a pendulum from one extreme to another or surrender to chronic burnout, accepting that this is just what motherhood feels like.

We spread on yet another layer of the guilt and shame because *shouldn't we be doing this better?* We're told that motherhood is magical, so why does it feel hard? Isn't there a better way? Shouldn't we be able to find a way to care for ourselves and fill ourselves back up so we can experience all the bliss motherhood has to offer? Shouldn't we be drinking the green smoothies, working out, getting our nails done, and looking presentable? Shouldn't we be starting small businesses based on our passions while also planning the birthday parties and baking the organic, gluten-free, grain-free, vegan cupcakes? Shouldn't we be able to *be it all* and *do it all* without feeling the weight of it all?

The illusion that there's a perfect, achievable balance sets mothers up to feel like we're getting it all wrong because we haven't discovered the "right" way. We begin believing that if we just google the right combination of words, find the right Instagram post, or mix the right ratio of fats and carbs, we'll reach the victorious, self-actualized place that is balance.

I want to give you a clear statement to hold close to your heart. If that doesn't work, you can tattoo it on your forehead. The statement is simple: *balance is baloney.*

Let it go! Set that myth straight and know that achieving the ultimate, perfect, and permanent balance isn't the goal—nor is it a realistic outcome to aim for. Feeling like you're out of whack, falling short, or behind is completely normal and to be expected.

Please, stop internalizing this imbalance as an implication that you're not measuring up or that you're not "enough." This tendency in motherhood is severely detrimental to your self-concept and quality of life. The goal isn't to achieve a balanced resting state; instead, it's knowing how to easily recalibrate your day-to-day life. This knowledge will take you from feeling like you're frazzled and falling short to feeling equipped and at peace.

———

I knew when I came out of my haze that I wanted to find a way to help moms navigate motherhood differently. This is my *why*. When I emerged many years and a son (Roy) later, I dug into research, books, and blogs and pulled from my expertise from working in the relationship education field for over fifteen years to compile what I am sharing with you in this book.

Rather than telling you to seek balance, I'll teach you how to quickly make micro-adjustments in your relationship with yourself. I also want to make a promise to you about the pages that follow: I won't waste your time. You'll find practical and helpful information in these chapters that will change the way you experience motherhood. You'll gain new insight into how to navigate the age-old conflict we women face: Do I sacrifice myself for the kids or sacrifice my kids for the preservation of myself? (Hint: the answer isn't so black and white.)

You'll learn practical tools for

- staying connected to yourself,
- seeing yourself in a positive light and ditching the mom guilt for good,
- assessing and asserting your needs with confidence,
- prioritizing your relationships and responsibilities in ways that you can feel at peace with, and
- listening to your body when it's speaking to you.

You'll see that to really nourish your relationship with your kids, you must nourish your relationship with yourself.

This message is so close to my heart. It's the one I wished I had received in those early years of motherhood and am so grateful that I know it now as my kids are growing up. I'm so honored you're here; I know how valuable your time is, and I am really eager to share this message with you.

Let's do this.

*part one*

# how did we get here?

# *Chapter One*

## WE MOM SO HARD

I will never forget trying to pack up to take our youngest child, Roy, to his first pediatrician appointment shortly after he was born. I was barely able to find a moment to pull myself together. Our oldest, Effie, was two and a half, and she rattled off demands like an auctioneer. How could I possibly get dressed, let alone shower, breastfeed every two minutes, and meet the "needs" (I use that term loosely) of a toddler? Those were really my days at that time: meeting the demands of a relentlessly needy toddler and feeling the guilt when I was pulled in two directions. I felt constantly forced to choose between giving Effie attention to avoid her potential tantrum and giving attention to our newborn son. I was spinning and exhausted and burned-out.

When I finally sat down to speak with the pediatrician, frazzled and breaking a sweat, she took a look at his umbilical cord.

"Did you get this wet?" she asked.

"I don't know. He probably peed on it. I'm not used to changing a boy's diaper." I put my head down and felt my face get hot as the shame rushed in. Roy's umbilical cord was getting infected. I was a week in and already falling short as a mother of two kids.

The doctor smiled at me.

"It's okay; this happens a lot."

I appreciated her words, but they didn't do much to console my heart and mind. I had already concluded that I wasn't seamlessly transitioning into this role as I'd envisioned I would.

As we wrapped up the appointment, the pediatrician swiveled her chair toward me.

"Oh, one more thing. This can be a tough time for Effie, so try to get fifteen minutes a day of playtime with her."

"Excuse me, did you say fifty minutes?"

"Nope, fifteen."

I think, in that moment with all my newborn haze, I wasn't able to fully process the gravity of her statement. Had she just given me the most amazing gift of my life: permission to ease the heck up on my crazy standards? Fifteen minutes? Are you kidding me? I spent the majority of my day playing with our daughter while also trying to juggle a colicky newborn, stay on top of my work obligations, nurse, feed our family, not run out of toilet paper, and keep the home put together.

I wish I could tell you this message was my turning point and that I walked out of that office with a newfound freedom and lightness that forever changed my mothering experience.

But alas, I was hell-bent on being a mother who had it all together. My mantra was "I can do all the things and look good doing them. I won't lower my standards because that's weak and means I've given up and given in to the curse of mediocrity. I am woman; hear me roar."

So I left that appointment like the pack mule we all become in the beginning of motherhood. Armed with a car seat in one hand, a diaper bag slung over my shoulder, and a wailing toddler on my hip,

I felt ready to conquer this parenting business. I refused to risk the possibility of selling my two-and-a-half-year-old short. What if the doctor was wrong about fifteen minutes being all that Effie needed? How could I possibly take the chance of permanently affecting her in some negative capacity, such as stunting her emotional development or inflicting trauma she'd unpack in therapy twenty years from now? Put my kid's well-being on the line for some indulgent consideration of balance? Heck no!

My resistance to recalibrating my life and saving my sanity isn't unique to me. In fact, I'd bet the reason you're here is because this resembles your experience. This desire to feel better in motherhood—to feel free, untethered, and more like the former you—tugs at your soul, but your kids, your love for them, their needs, your guilt, and your sense of responsibility tug right back at your heart and mind.

I've spent a lot of time thinking about the undercurrents of our experiences in motherhood—those things that suck the joy out of it and fill us with guilt and shame and feelings of falling short. Throughout my study of the research and literature, it became clear to me that mothers contend with three primary conflicts that, if left undefined and unnamed, dramatically impact the motherhood experience. I want to offer you a new way forward that will not only dramatically change the way you feel in motherhood but ultimately will be better for you and your relationships.

## THE CONFLICTS ALL MOMS FACE

There are three core conflicts that define and shape the motherhood experience:

1. The Sacrifice of Your Identity: my needs versus the needs of everyone else

2. The Idealization of Motherhood: my ideals versus my reality
3. The Intensity of Your Parenting Standards: my parenting must be perfect versus my parenting is good enough

Most of the time these conflicts are just operating in the background, unbeknownst to us. They eat away at our confidence, whisper reminders of all the things we wish we'd done differently, and keep us "in line" when we attempt to care for ourselves. These conflicts create feelings of discomfort in motherhood, and we try to avoid that discomfort by altering our behaviors. This can look like overinvesting in our relationships, overcompensating with our kids to narrow the gap between our ideals and our reality, and overparenting to discharge the worry that we're totally messing up our kids. We think doing these things will make us feel better. But we don't. Instead, we feel depleted and weary.

When these core conflicts aren't named and defined, they operate like a nasty, hidden smell in your car. You can definitely tell something stinks, but you can't figure out where the smell's coming from, which means you can't get rid of it! Consider me your nose, sniffing out the conflicts that stink in motherhood.

## Core Conflict 1: The Sacrifice of Your Identity: My Needs Versus the Needs of Everyone Else

Navigating your needs versus the needs of your relationships is a tale as old as time for women. One central and defining aspect of becoming a mother is the idea that you have a moral obligation to self-sacrifice for the greater good of your family and children. We spend much of our youth and young adult life trying to understand and meet our needs, but once we become mothers, we begin believing our needs must almost cease to exist because we've been summoned to the higher purpose of motherhood.

I'm sure if you think about it, even just for a moment, you can recall messaging you've received about this "duty" to love your family well—even if it costs caring for yourself well. Throughout our lives we've been programmed with this messaging. Some of it is subtle, whereas other instances are more overt.

A perfect example of this happened when I was talking to my mom on the phone. My mother-in-law had been in the hospital for over a week, and her condition wasn't improving. In the past eight months, she'd had two knee-replacement surgeries and a gallbladder removal, and she was now in the hospital for pancreatitis. Understandably, my mother-in-law was fed up. During our conversation, I mentioned to my mom that I wanted to send my mother-in-law something. She'd been through so much, but flowers seemed pointless.

"How about you send your father-in-law dinner? I mean, what is he even doing for food?"

When she said this, something inside me exploded. In that moment, my mother-in-law lay frustrated and hopeless in the hospital, and even my own mother (a strong woman who advocates for me to assert my needs) was suggesting that I send a gift to the husband. There was an assumption in my mom's suggestion that what my mother-in-law needed most wasn't something for her but rather something to ensure her loved ones were okay. This is a perfect example of messaging that says our needs should be less important or nonexistent. If you start to pay attention, you'll see similar messages everywhere.

Harriet Lerner wrote about this in her bestselling book *The Dance of Anger* as "de-selfing." She said, "'De-selfing' means that one's self, including one's thoughts, wants, beliefs, and ambitions, is 'negotiable' under pressures from the relationship."[1] In other words, when women feel their relationships will suffer if they prioritize themselves, they sacrifice their own needs, desires, and wants to preserve the well-being of the relationship.

Emily and Amelia Nagoski also talk about this phenomenon

in their book *Burnout*, where they use the term "Human Giver Syndrome."

Human givers are those who have a moral obligation to give their humanity to the human *beings*. Human givers feel they must be small and needless, caretakers, not too ambitious or emotional or demanding—and, surely, they shouldn't inconvenience others.[2]

Does this sound familiar?

In so many ways women have been taught to nurture their relationships over themselves. One of the most impactful ways this shows up in motherhood is in all the responsibilities that require physical and cognitive effort that we pile on. Eve Rodsky's *Fair Play* perfectly captured this experience by calling women the "she-fault partner" in relationships, meaning women are the ones who tend to be the default person who takes care of all the things and all the people.[3] This is the mental load also referred to as "invisible labor" or "invisible load." This isn't just an issue of inequality within the home. The invisible load is also a deeply rooted pattern of generations of women taking care of their homes and family members' needs at the expense of themselves, their sanity, and—oftentimes— their happiness in motherhood and marriage.

In most of the books I've read on motherhood, there are vast descriptions of patriarchy, cultural shifts, and theories on why they exist.[4] This isn't one of those books. The reason why is because those books have already been written, and when I read them, I sometimes feel helpless. How can I *feel* better if I can't immediately go fix society? I wanted to offer moms something that they can implement in their lives and homes right away. However, we can't talk about motherhood without acknowledging this major truth: women are most often the ones who fulfill the "human giver" role. Women are the ones who tend to "de-self" in order to care for their relationships. Women, almost always, take on the role as nurturer, relationship manager, and default parent.

This tendency to de-self is so deeply ingrained in us that we wear it as a badge of honor. We can even perpetuate the messaging in the narratives we form about ourselves and about mothers we perceive as stepping out of line by not de-selfing. For example, think about *that* mom: she looks put together all the time, she always has her nails done, or she seems "too indulgent" by frequently going to yoga. On the surface, we commend her for how she's able to care for herself, but then we give her the stink eye behind her back.

We do this to ourselves too. If we tip the scales a bit and take a moment for ourselves, we tend to judge our own actions in the same way. *What kind of mom would leave her kids for that long? What kind of mom would drop her two-year-old off at preschool? That's too young.* Why do we do this? Because this conflict between how we invest in ourselves versus how we invest in our other relationships runs deep. The messaging that it's our moral obligation to de-self for the greater good of our relationships has been ingrained in us for generations.

I want to mention that this capacity to care so deeply and selflessly for our relationships is a beautiful aspect of women. We're exceptionally equipped in this way. However, when motherhood hits, responsibilities skyrocket, and free time is hard to come by, it becomes even harder to determine who should get priority. Herein lies the crux of the conflict we face in motherhood: Who's to be sacrificed—you or your kids?

When we throw ourselves fully into our kids, we burn out, develop resentment, and feel discontentment with life. When we put ourselves at the forefront of our lives, we also feel terrible things like shame, guilt, and worry that we're missing out on those special moments with our kids. Finding a balance of priorities feels futile.

This conflict is one I struggled with as I prepared to go to the pediatrician's office that day many years ago. Our daughter literally made her demands loud and clear, and I shrank my needs to meet hers. I, like so many other moms, felt consumed by my identity as a mother, and it didn't feel good.

In my study and research, I've discovered that there is another way. We have more to choose from than just the two extremes of self-abandonment or child-abandonment. Our relationship with our children is symbiotic; we're interconnected, and there's opportunity for both to thrive. We'll dive more into this later.

## Core Conflict 2: The Idealization of Motherhood: My Ideals Versus My Reality

Have you ever noticed that pictures posted to Instagram of moms crying seem to perform really well? You know the picture: a mom is sitting outside somewhere like the grocery store—maybe holding her baby over her shoulder (or with the baby in the background)—and she has red eyes with tears streaming down her face. It's an honest and real glimpse into motherhood. The likes and reassuring comments pour in. Why? Because there's deep messaging in our society that motherhood is magical, that it's the pinnacle of our lives and completes us as women. Yet when we actually become mothers and are immersed in the fog of no sleep, self-doubt, lack of freedom, and guilt about our own needs, we feel completely and utterly confused. These pictures are momentary reprieves from the confusion because they remind us and reassure us that we're not alone in this experience.

I once posted a question to Instagram, asking my community about the messages about motherhood they'd received before they became mothers. Hundreds of direct messages poured in. I read stories of moms who expected to feel love at first sight for their baby but experienced numbness and postpartum depression instead. Some moms expected a baby with a calm temperament but instead were faced with the reality of a colicky newborn. Other moms thought they'd feel a sense of mother's intuition that just never showed up after giving birth. Many moms expected motherhood to complete a part of them, but they instead discovered motherhood felt really hard. Motherhood can be draining, and it often leaves moms feeling like a hint of their former selves, rather than the actualized version they hoped to become.

I know I had a very clear vision of the mother I would eventually be. Scenes would play out like a movie in my mind. I did this all the time. I have an entire mental film collection of my ideal motherhood moments. I'll share one of my movies with you; I've titled it "The Fun Mom: *Little House on the Prairie* Edition." It goes something like this: I'm walking through my farmhouse kitchen wearing a beautiful floral housedress that shows no hint of previously birthing a child. My hair is effortlessly swept into a bun with the perfect pieces falling down, framing my face. I'm barefoot, duh, and walking toward our young daughter, where she's waiting for me at the end of the counter. Her hair is in pigtails, and she's dressed tastefully in neutral tones, wearing a tiny-size apron that must have been ordered on Etsy. She is perched on a stool holding a wooden spoon, ready to stir the rest of the ingredients in a scalloped-edge, robin's-egg blue bowl that perfectly suits my farmhouse kitchen. I carry a glass jar of flour over to her, dip my finger in the flour, and wipe some on her cheek. She giggles and a flour-throwing party ensues in the kitchen. We start laughing hysterically as puffs of white flour fill the kitchen, and we break into a slow-motion dance scene and "My Girl" (or something nostalgic) plays in the background. End scene.

Here's the thing: I don't have a farmhouse kitchen. But if I did, I would be so worried about flour getting into the crevices of my vintage farmhouse floors and having the energy left over, after baking with a toddler, to clean up the mess we made making this movie-worthy memory. It just wouldn't happen. My reality was more like a tired mom in sweats, on day three of not washing my hair so it's crunchy and up in a messy bun, trying to be "chill" while my three-year-old wants to run the mixer and keeps eating all the chocolate chips, so I'm internally freaking out at the sugar tantrum that's surely coming for me in the next hour. My anxiety would be increasing, my energy would be dwindling, and it most definitely would not end in a slow-motion dance party.

I could go on endlessly with these scenes I created in my mind. They were all so far from my reality that I spent a great deal of my time in early motherhood feeling like I was doing it all wrong or missing out on creating magical moments. Unfortunately, dissatisfaction, hurt, and self-doubt occur in the gap between our ideals and our reality. I'm sure, like me, you can identify areas of motherhood in which your ideals are far from your reality.

This mismatch between cultural messages that idealize motherhood and the reality of our experiences is a breeding ground for feelings of inadequacy. Most of us believe we're falling short, and we're desperate for reassurance that we're not alone in our experience.

Our ideals about motherhood are largely shaped by culture, by our early caregivers, and by our relationship experiences. These ideals cover a vast number of categories, from the type of mother we imagine we'll be, to the type of child we believe we'll have, to how easy or hard parenting will feel. The chapters that follow will cover this conflict in more depth, but we must first recognize that it exists. We're regularly carrying two realities in our hearts and minds that feel conflicting: *that motherhood is amazing and that motherhood is really hard*. Managing these conflicting realities uses our bandwidth and has a powerful impact on our day-to-day lived experiences in motherhood.

## Core Conflict 3: The Intensity of Your Parenting Standards: My Parenting Must Be Perfect Versus My Parenting Is Good Enough

The gist of the third conflict is this: as moms, we're encouraged to devote an inordinate amount of time, money, and energy into the development and care of our children while simultaneously being subjected to increased judgment (from ourselves and others) and feelings of comparison with other women. All of this inevitably leads to weariness and the worry that we never really measure up. However, when we seek to ease up and parent less intensively, we feel a rush of guilt and shame. It's the hamster wheel of motherhood. How can we get off this crazy-making cycle without experiencing major consequences?

In 1996, Sharon Hays coined the term "intensive mothering." She defined five key tenets to this ideology:

1. ESSENTIALISM: the belief that mothers are the most important or essential parent
2. FULFILLMENT: the belief that parents should be fulfilled by their children
3. STIMULATION: the belief that involved parents should provide consistent intellectual stimulation for their children
4. CHILD-CENTERED: the belief that the parents' lives should revolve around their children
5. CHALLENGING: the belief that parenting is hard and draining[5]

Do any of these feel familiar? Numerous studies have been conducted on the concept of intensive mothering and have found, not surprisingly, that this ideology results in increased stress and guilt, less satisfaction with life, and a feeling of being burdened by motherhood. Furthermore, intensive mothering qualities were studied in regard to mental health outcomes like depression, stress, and life satisfaction. The three most impactful dimensions of intensive parenting on mental health outcomes were essentialism, challenging, and child-centered.[6]

This just makes common sense; if you believe that you, as the mother, are the most important and essential parent, it will be difficult for you to involve support and childcare. Because how could you, in good conscience, put your kids in the hands of second-rate caregivers? So moms who ascribe to this belief don't tend to ask for or accept help. Or when they do, they are overwhelmed with guilt for doing so. This creates a lose-lose situation. This also increases something called *maternal gatekeeping behaviors*, which is a mother's protective belief about how much parenting and childcare responsibility to turn over to the other parent. Maternal gatekeeping tends to restrict co-parenting efforts and ultimately sabotage a mother's mental health, even setting her up to carry more of the mental load later in the relationship.[7] Buying into the essentialism belief ultimately "increases stress and lowers life satisfaction among women as they focus more on caring for their children than themselves."[8]

The "challenging" ideology also makes sense. If you believe parenting is difficult and stressful, you will experience more difficulty and stress (see more in chapter 8). Now, we all know parenting is difficult at times, but holding this belief as a central and defining aspect of motherhood can erode feelings of confidence and impact your mental health.

The final ideology that showed the most impact for moms was "child-centered." As I've discussed already, we moms already tend to be the human givers. We tend to be the de-selfers and the she-faults. The last thing we need is feelings of guilt and shame when we do something that doesn't put our children at the center of our world. One of the most difficult aspects of becoming a mother is the loss of freedom.[9] This ideology fuels that loss. If we believe we must revolve our lives around our children, we lose the ability to step out of that constraining bubble and do something for ourselves. This belief also sabotages asking for help and involving support. We weren't meant to mother this way, and the impact of intensive mothering has not been good for our mental health or the joy we feel in motherhood.

One of the key takeaways from the research on intensive mothering is that mothering in itself may not be the direct cause of depression, stress, and decreased life satisfaction, but rather it's signing on to these beliefs and the behaviors that support intensive *ways* of mothering that relate to these negative outcomes.

Mothering didn't always look this way. Allow me to give you a brief overview of how we got here.

There was a marked shift in parenting in the late 1940s and early 1950s. Prior to then, parenting advice was largely concerned with children being spoiled. Behavioral psychologists like John Watson argued that children didn't need much attention or affection and that overindulgent parenting would mess up children.

In 1946, Dr. Benjamin Spock published *The Common Sense Book of Baby and Child Care* and argued a totally different perspective on parenting. He suggested that the core of good parenting was attending to your kids' needs carefully at their different stages of development.

Right on the heels of Spock's book was the introduction of one of the most prominent theories in psychology: attachment theory. Attachment theory, pioneered by John Bowlby in the late 1950s, found that the way early caregivers respond to infants' needs forms the templates for how the infants will attach in their relationships throughout the course of their lives. Guess who the main caregivers usually are? Yep, moms! Talk about some serious pressure! You, the mother, have the power to impact *all* of your kids' relationships throughout the course of their *entire* lives based on how you respond to their needs as an infant. No pressure.

These two major landmarks in parenting history shifted the narrative around mothering and rearing children. Kids are not, in fact, little adults; they're delicate creatures we have major influence over. We can help them thrive or completely thwart their growth. This was the beginning of a domino effect in how we parent and the intentionality and intensity with which we raise our children. Don't get me wrong—these shifts were important and positive; however, the pendulum began to swing from detached parenting to intense, hypervigilant parenting.

Moms, we're faced with an unwinnable situation. Do we turn down the intensity and face ridicule and judgment from others or from ourselves? Or do we continue with this intensity, burnout, and struggle to enjoy motherhood?

Susan Douglas and Meredith Michaels, authors of *The Mommy Myth*, described intensive mothering so well:

> Intensive mothering insists that mothers acquire professional-level skills such as those of a therapist, pediatrician, consumer products safety inspector, and teacher, and that they lavish every ounce of physical vitality they have, the monetary equivalent of the gross domestic product of Australia, and most of all, every single bit of their emotional, mental, and psychic energy on their kids. We must learn to put on the masquerade of the doting, self-sacrificial mother and wear it at all times. With intensive mothering, everyone watches us, we watch ourselves, and other mothers, and we watch ourselves watching ourselves.[10]

I faced this intensive mothering struggle when the pediatrician suggested that our daughter only needed fifteen minutes of play together. How could I fulfill my obligation to parent intensely while easing up and doing less? The trade-off of parenting less intensely would be that I might experience feelings of falling short or guilt. However, if we look at our generation of mothers objectively, we clearly can conclude that we mom so hard, and our kids aren't likely suffering from any lack of intention, care, love, or time.

For example, did you know moms today who juggle full-time jobs outside the home spend just as much time tending to their children as stay-at-home mothers did in the 1970s?[11] Can you seriously just sit with that fun little fact for a minute until you can feel the relief sweep through your body?

The next time you've spent what feels like a lifetime on the floor playing LEGOS with your kid, just to feel completely guilt-ridden later when you need to answer some emails, remember you probably just spent more quality time with your kid in that moment than moms in the 1970s did in a week.

Research on the millennial mother echoes what I'm guessing you experience: mothers judge themselves more harshly than previous generations, and they are judged more harshly than previous generations.[12] As the first generation to parent in a social media age, parenting has never been more open to public criticism as well as affirmation. A BabyCenter survey of moms found that 83 percent of the respondents said it was important to them to be the "perfect mother."[13]

You may read this and roll your eyes—who really thinks we can actually be perfect mothers? It's inconceivable (said in the voice from *The Princess Bride*)! But I ask you to really take inventory of how you live as a mother. Do you believe perfection is impossible while you unconsciously strive every day to achieve it (and feel like crap when you don't)?

The millennial generation, in general, is obsessed with self-improvement and with being their best selves. In fact, they spend twice the amount of money on personal care and improvement as boomers and make more "personal improvement commitments than any generation before them."[14] Don't believe me? Just take a look at the online course options that are available these days! Want to learn to raise chickens? There's a course for that. Do you need to heal your inner child? Take your pick. Do you want something on meditation and deep breathing? The options are endless.

To be clear, I'm not knocking this quest for self-actualization. I live in the self-help and education world. It's my livelihood. However, it's important to realize and take comfort in the fact that this mentality has flowed into how we mother and has dialed up our felt pressure to parent more intensely—and the impact is palpable.

The bright side of what we learn from survey data on millennials is that we really value being moms. Some have even suggested we're the most family-friendly generation yet, and 93 percent of parents surveyed said being seen as a "good" parent by their spouse is extremely important to them.[15]

The bottom line is that we're highly invested in being good moms; we want to do a good job. In fact, we take it to another level in that we consider parenting our first priority and part of our core identity—93 percent of moms say that being a mother is "extremely" or "very" important to their identity.[16]

So what does this all really mean in practical terms? It means we mother in such a way that our kids, and all outcomes associated with them, are extensions of us. Our parenting has become an expression of ourselves. This sounds beautiful, self-sacrificial, and almost poetic, but there's a dark side to it. When our kids lose it, we feel like it means we totally suck. Or if we have a child with a temperament that's harder to navigate, it feels like we're constantly failing. Or if our kid develops anxiety, we believe we're somehow responsible.

One of the most profound parts of motherhood is the loss of self-preoccupation. However, if we consider our children as an extension of ourselves (whether consciously or through lived-out actions), we've actually become intensely self-preoccupied. This means that everything our kids do is a direct reflection of either our competency or incompetency as mothers.

The message we've all received loud and clear is that our kids are living proof of how good of a mother we are. We must train hard for this role and perform at all costs. This is the difficult mix of feelings that accompanies this conflict. We want to feel light and joyful, but when our "enoughness" is tethered to the outcomes associated with our kids, we're in for a roller-coaster ride of highs and lows.

## THE WAY FORWARD

Combine the conflicting messages of motherhood with the myth that we can achieve some perfect balance, like I mentioned in "Balance Is

Baloney," and it's clear why we feel like we're falling short. There's inevitable exhaustion in trying to be everything to everyone. We're under immense pressure to do it all well. We're doing a great job as mothers, we're pouring into our kids in major ways, but we're doing it at the expense of ourselves.

Please hear this loud and clear: we can't parent our kids with intention and care while abandoning ourselves for the cause. To truly care well for our children, we must care well for ourselves. My hope is that this chapter has reassured you that you already have the "caring well" for your children down. If you were up for a motherhood review, you'd most definitely receive an "exceeds expectations." The piece that's missing is how to care well for your kids without neglecting yourself.

> **We can't parent our kids with intention and care while abandoning ourselves for the cause.**

You already empower your kids to know themselves, listen to their intuition, and explore their passions; there's a way for you to know yourself, listen to your intuition, and explore your passion too. You already guide your kids to have a positive belief in themselves; there's a way for you to see yourself in a positive light too. You already help your kids identify and honor their emotions; there's a way for you to tune in to your emotions with compassion and care too. You already encourage your kids to prioritize and assert their needs; there's a way for you to prioritize your needs too. You already teach your kids the power of making and keeping promises; there's a way to keep promises to yourself too. You already help your kids care for their bodies; there's a way for you to honor and nourish your body too.

The way forward isn't a perfect balance. It's not about behaving perfectly in an attempt to resolve the conflicts we've struggled with in motherhood. Instead, it's about adopting one simple decree: *care for yourself the same way you care for your children.*

Most moms are naturally the managers of relationships. We are the ones who do the heavy lifting in our relationships: checking in on our partners, worrying about our kids, becoming experts in our families and intuiting their needs. However, we sort of stink at doing these things for ourselves. Imagine how cared for we'd feel if we took this incredible skill set and turned it toward us. We must learn to mother ourselves like we mother our kids.

Rest assured—I know you don't have a surplus of time, and your plate is already beyond full. I know you don't need more to do or carry around in your mind. Part of what makes motherhood so hard is that when we feel drained and overwhelmed, we don't know *how* to feel better.

I will give you a clear plan of action, with things you can do in mere moments, that can fit seamlessly into your routine or be squeezed in between diaper changes. The approach I'm offering in this book is targeted and efficient because I know that's what you need most.

I know you'll also need convincing that you deserve care. I know you'll struggle to assert your needs and shift your self-concept. I know you won't want to inconvenience your family in order to find time for you. This book will address all these concerns (and then some), and it will be a place you can return to when you need to be reminded of why caring for yourself is important for you *and* for those you love.

*Chapter Two*

# MOTHER YOURSELF LIKE
# YOU MOTHER YOUR KIDS

**M**y close friend and I were perched at my kitchen island. We assumed our positions on the same stools our butts have graced a million times during playdates over the years. We always sat there to be available for the inevitable snack requests and squabbles.

Mid-conversation, she looked at me with total conviction: "I know that there won't be an ideal time for me to go back to school, but I can't sideline myself any longer. I was okay with it for a time, but now I'm done."

Her husband travels constantly for work, and much of her life and routine are pieced together around his. She's the ultimate accommodator and has worn this role with grace. She'd recently decided to start a master's degree program and was telling me about the difficulty in navigating her new schedule.

This resolve to prioritize her needs didn't happen overnight. My friend, much like me, took her time—and she experienced pain, struggle, and sacrifice as a result. Finally, she was ready to claim her place as a separate, important, and worthy member of her family who deserved to nourish herself. She'd been consciously devoting herself to all her other relationships, but she knew in her heart and soul that she couldn't continue to give without tending to her own needs.

Making the decision to care for ourselves isn't easy; when we start to prioritize our needs, there is often an inner resistance that beckons us to go back to the status quo. I will talk more about the pain and resistance of prioritizing yourself in chapter 7. Know that making these shifts can be difficult, but in the end they are growing pains that are so worth enduring.

When I put forth the rule to *mother yourself like you mother your kids*, I knew you'd need some convincing that you deserve this type of care. My friend didn't come to this conclusion immediately either. She needed to see that caring for her own well-being was essential—it affected every one of her relationships, not just her relationship with herself.

Mothering yourself like you mother your kids is important for a few reasons:

1. When you don't care for yourself, you burn out.
2. Being a *good-enough* mom is actually better than being a *perfect* mom.
3. Your relationships flourish only when you do too.
4. Your relationship with your children is mutually beneficial.

This chapter is the presentation of my case for your care. Like a personal defense attorney, I will appeal to your rational, scientific, and emotional mind and convince you that despite the discomfort it may cause you, your well-being is of the utmost importance.

# WHY MOTHER YOURSELF?

## 1. When you don't care for yourself, you burn out.

A 2020 Motherly survey of over 3,800 moms looked at how moms were doing over the prior year in several major categories (March 2019–March 2020). Some of the key findings were that 41 percent of mothers felt burnout frequently or all the time. Only 8 percent of them reported getting eight hours of sleep per night. Sixty-eight percent said that in the last day they had less than an hour to themselves without work or family obligations. Fifty-one percent of these mothers said they hadn't had a date night with their partner in the last month.[1] I doubt that these findings shock you—you are here reading this book after all.

You don't have to look far to see the theme of "burned-out mother" because it populates mainstream media, as it did particularly during the COVID-19 pandemic. The *New York Times* even did an entire series on the state of motherhood called *The Primal Scream*, which outlined the struggles of modern motherhood.[2] The series highlighted inequitable distribution of the invisible labor, the sacrifice mothers make leaving the workforce, and the lack of structural and societal support for both working and stay-at-home mothers. The series' central theme showed that mothers across the board aren't receiving enough support and that we're burning out and suffering because of it.

Burnout is a state characterized by three major symptoms:

1. emotional and physical exhaustion ("I'm burned-out"),
2. depersonalization or disconnecting from yourself and others ("I'm numbing out"), and
3. impairment in regulating either emotional or cognitive processes ("I'm losing it").

In real life, burnout shows up as day-to-day issues that we can all relate to: less creative energy, forgetfulness, physical pain and exhaustion, emotional sensitivity, irritability, impatience, anxiety, and feeling overwhelmed.

In *Burnout*, Emily and Amelia Nagoski define *burnout* as getting stuck in the middle of a stress response.[3] Essentially, it's lingering in a chronic and activated state of stress for a prolonged period of time. This has significant effects on the individual's physical, emotional, mental, and relational health.

People who report experiencing burnout have higher rates of physical health issues, including heart disease, muscle tension, autoimmune issues, gastrointestinal issues, headaches, and sleep disturbances. They experience greater rates of depression and mood disorders. The relationships of individuals who experience burnout also tend to suffer. While strong support and healthy relationships can be protective and aid in recovering from burnout, these relationships can also deteriorate because of it.[4]

Burnout is too common among mothers. You can't run yourself ragged for the sake of your loved ones just to suffer in silence or, worse, suffer so dramatically that you're unable to show up for your loved ones. You must mother yourself like you mother your kids so you can safeguard yourself from burnout—the price of your physical, emotional, mental, and relational health is too high.

## 2. Being a good-enough mom is actually better than being a perfect mom.

In 1953, pediatrician and psychoanalyst D. W. Winnicott coined the term "good-enough mother." His message was simple: to raise a psychologically healthy child, you don't need to be perfect; you just need to be good enough. In fact, he argued that a perfect mother could actually be detrimental to a child's development.[5] Why? Because we live in an imperfect world. Our job as mothers isn't to be our children's personal butler (much to my children's chagrin) or to shield them from challenges but rather to equip them to exist in a world that can be difficult. Our job is to meet their needs consistently as infants and then to pull back on our intensity. The best thing we can do is provide a safe and loving landing spot when our kids need it.

I'll never forget driving home after a Memorial Day party as our daughter was crying hysterically in the back seat. She was begging me to give in to her request so that she wouldn't feel disappointment. During that drive home I said one of the most important strings of words I've uttered to my daughter in her short eight years.

"Effie, I love you. It's painful as your mom to see you feel anything hard. But if I protect you from all your hard feelings, then you won't believe in your own ability to handle hard feelings. It's my job to prepare you for all parts of your life, and that includes helping you know you're fully capable of handling difficult things. You're strong enough."

Surprisingly, it worked. Usually my skill set as a therapist is lost on my kids, and they tune me out. But this time, it sunk in. She understood.

The perfection-striving part of me wanted to rescue my daughter and make it all better. Plus, it would've made for a calmer ride home. But in my "perfection," I'd ultimately be doing her a major disservice. There's something very powerful about not being perfect.

D. W. Winnicott offered cautionary wisdom—and much-needed permission—when he reassured moms that they don't need to parent their kids so intensely. We can let them have the space to learn that they are resilient. We can allow them to struggle in manageable ways and offer loving support when they need it so they can thrive in an imperfect and often frustrating world.

Research on topics like the development of resilience and grit, as well as research on intensive parenting, highlight the detrimental effects of parenting too intensely. For example, a 2012 study of 438 college students found that intensive parenting was linked to problematic development in young adults, primarily because they didn't develop the important skills to become self-reliant adults.[6] Another 2013 study of 297 college students found that students with helicopter parents had higher levels of depression and lower levels of life satisfaction. Researchers attributed this to a violation of the students' basic needs for autonomy and the development of competence.[7]

I realize these studies may amplify your worry about messing up your kids. That isn't the intention; rather, it's to reassure you that extreme overinvestment in your kids isn't the answer. You don't need to make everything feel easy for your kids. You don't need to give your entire self to your kids in order for them to be whole. In fact, for them to develop wholly, you *can't* give all of yourself.

Furthermore, being the "perfect" or "intensive" mother doesn't offer a healthy model for your kids. This precedent shows kids that they must self-deprive in order to care for others, and I'm sure you don't wish that for your sons or daughters.

I know you care deeply about doing the best and being the best for your kids. Take peace in knowing that good-enough mothering really *is* good enough.

## 3. Your relationships flourish only when you do.

My husband travels a lot for work, which I hate and love at the same time. The kids and I miss him like crazy, which is the hate part, but the alone time I get is life-giving. I can do minimal cooking, pick at pimples, and go to bed red-faced and spotty. I can stay up way too late, turn the TV up loud, and watch whatever I want! This isn't really any different from when he's home, but it *feels* different. This brings me to a few weeks ago, when I was totally alone and decided to watch a documentary called *Intelligent Trees*.

This documentary depicts the work of Suzanne Simard, an ecologist from the University of British Columbia. A little fun fact for you: her work was the inspiration behind the tree of souls in the movie

*Avatar.* What Simard found in her research is that trees are social and relational beings. They communicate with one another through a complex system of roots and mycorrhizal fungi networks. Trees are able to recognize their kin and provide their saplings with the nutrients they need through these networks. Even more incredible, when trees are struggling, they communicate through these networks, hilariously (if you're into puns) coined the "wood-wide web." Through this system of connection, the trees send nutrients to the sickly trees.[8]

An essential part of these forest networks is the "mother trees." Mother trees are the oldest and biggest trees, and they're the glue holding the forest together. They have massive photosynthetic capacity and provide food for the whole soil network. Mother trees keep carbon in the soil and above ground, help water flow properly, aid in caring for sickly trees, and help the forest recover when it's suffered major disturbances. Mother trees are said to be so essential to the ecosystem that "we cannot afford to lose them." If mother trees are lost, the rest of the forest will deteriorate.[9]

A defining feature of mother trees is their stature. They're the biggest, oldest, and sturdiest trees. They stand mighty in the forest. If they were small and stunted, they wouldn't be life-giving and life-sustaining.

You are much the same as these mother trees. You're undoubtedly deeply rooted and connected to your family and those you love, sending your life force out to give life to others. But are you standing mighty? You see, if you aren't, it's not just you who's at stake—it's your entire network. How can you give what you don't have? How can you care for those you love when you're depleted? You can't afford to be deprived.

Your strength and mightiness will breed the same traits in those you love. Your relationship with your children is symbiotic. You grow strong, and they grow strong. You give to yourself, and you can better give to them. Don't ever underestimate the importance of growing powerful and resilient. I know you worry about being self-ish, taking more time than you feel you deserve, needing too much, or inconveniencing others—but remember that the vitality and well-being of your network requires that you're nourished, flourishing, and healthy. In short, to be mighty in motherhood, you must mother yourself like you mother your kids.

## 4. Your relationship with your children is mutually beneficial.

Allow me to take you back to sixth grade science and define sym-biotic relationships. Symbiotic relationships exist when two species live close together, and there are two common types: mutualism and parasitism.

Let's be honest, if I asked you which of these terms best describes a mother-child relationship, you'd say parasitism, right? In fact, I've read a number of books on motherhood describing children in this exact way. The parasites take away the life from the life givers, and motherhood takes more than it gives.

We see messages on social media all the time that tell us mother-hood is the thief of our femininity, our appearance, our excitement, our sexiness, and our freedom. Just take a moment to scroll the mom memes, like the "Moma Lisa" who looks disheveled and worn down or the meme of Gollum from *The Lord of the Rings* with the text "after a day alone with the kids." Listen, I love a good meme, yet there's truth in just about every joke.

When we consume so much of this information—especially when we are caught in a moment of feeling worn down or find our-selves in the space between who we are and what we think we should be—what message is continually enforced? That motherhood took something from us we can't get back, that we're worse off for it, and that it's hard and draining. Does this doctrine serve us?

It's true we've all felt these things from time to time, and we'll likely feel them again. How could we not? Many of us grew these little humans in our bodies, and some of us fed them from our bodies, sacrificing our energy to provide them with theirs. We lose sleep for them. We give so much. I get it, the "parasite" analogy sometimes fits. But I ask you this: If we treat our relationships with our children as parasitic, how do we conceptualize caring for ourselves? Does that mean we care for ourselves only because it allows us to give more to our kids? That pouring into our own cups is only necessary for emptying them again? No thanks! That sounds exhausting.

Let's consider a mutually symbiotic relationship, a relationship in which both parties benefit. An example of this is bees and flowers. Bees take the nectar from the flowers and use it to make honey and food for the hive. The flowers are pollinated and multiply as the bees jump from bloom to bloom. Both the flowers and the bees benefit.

What if our relationships with our children were conceptualized this way? We tend to think of our kids as the flowers passively doing their thing while we buzz around doing the heavy lifting. What we know from science is that both the flowers and the bees have evolved over time to better work together. A recent study found that flowers can actually hear the sounds of buzzing, and in turn, their nectar becomes sweeter. Flowers also change shades of color to attract bees when they need to be pollinated the most. Did you know that bees have evolved to have longer tongues so they can better reach the nectar? Both bees and flowers have evolved because of the relationship they share together.[10] Motherhood isn't any different.

Abigail Tucker discussed the physiological side of this in her book *Mom Genes*. Tucker talked about groundbreaking science revealing that when mothers develop a disastrous condition called peripartum cardiomyopathy during pregnancy, 50 percent of them spontaneously recover. This recovery happens because the fetal cells from the unborn baby make their way to the mother's heart and repair the tissue.[11] In fact, a decade-long Dutch study tracked

190 women in their fifties and sixties and found that women who had detectable leftover fetal cells were less likely to die of virtually everything.[12] Babies aren't the parasites we've been told; in actuality, they're repairing our tissue and leaving behind bits of themselves to protect us while we're nourishing and growing their developing bodies.

From a psychological perspective, children have something to offer too. I know that, throughout my short time as a mother, my children have inadvertently shined light on parts of myself that could've easily remained in the dark. I know I've had to evolve generally as a person and specifically as a woman because of who I want to be for our daughter and what I want to demonstrate for our son.

Moms, we have a profoundly important choice. We can view motherhood as parasitic or mutualistic. We can view motherhood as an expansion of what we can become or as a restriction of who we already are. Motherhood can be a pathway of meaning-making or life-taking.

> **Motherhood can be a pathway of meaning-making or life-taking.**

You see, our relationship with our children isn't one-sided. We don't just pour into them without getting anything in return. Moms and kids are designed to grow from one another, evolve in important ways, and become better than we could ever be on our own. However, to realize this potential, we can't wither away into mere remnants of ourselves. We must nurture and care for ourselves so that we're thriving members of the relationships with our kids.

## ARE YOU CONVINCED?

I've always been good at picking up on people's vibes. If I had to describe the vibe of moms when we're offered clichés about self-care, being enough, or even prioritizing ourselves, the vibe is a half smile and noncommittal nod. It's the kind of vibe of paying lip service, but you know they have no intention of making any changes. Actually, *they* know they have no intention of making changes. It's a courtesy nod and smile with no real conviction behind it.

My hope is to push you beyond that courtesy nod and persuade you that not only is caring for yourself incredibly important for you, but it's absolutely essential for your other relationships to thrive.

I hope these words transform your feelings of hesitation and fast-track them into the absolute certainty that when you mother yourself like you mother your kids, you're doing the right thing for everyone.

## YOUR PLAN FOR BEING MIGHTY IN MOTHERHOOD

The remainder of this book will show you how to care for yourself in a way that's different from books that have come before. I promise that I won't just give you a massive list of self-care strategies—moms don't need more lists of things to do with the time they don't have!

Instead, I'll give you an integrated model that will help you understand the five bonds at the core of all your relationships. In the following chapters, you'll be introduced to the Relationship Attachment Model. The RAM is a picture of your relationship with your kids and the bonds that produce feelings of closeness and distance. It's also a picture of your relationship with yourself. Because the same bonds are part of all relationships—including the one with yourself—the RAM can be used as a window into your relationship with your kids *and* as a mirror reflecting back to you the areas in which you may need some attention and nurturing. This model will dramatically change how you think and feel about yourself and your relationships.

The RAM will give you clarity, empowering and emboldening you to check in with yourself in a targeted and efficient way and to make small shifts that will create massive changes in your relationship with yourself. When you can define the invisible obstacles and challenges you face in motherhood, you'll be able to take hold of your experience as a mom, implementing changes in specific and meaningful ways. This framework will help you feel differently in your life and in your mothering. In the next chapters, I'll help you understand the RAM and walk you through how to apply this model to yourself as you already do for your kids.

*Chapter Three*

# CREATE LASTING CONNECTION

Throughout this book I share stories about my mother and loads of stories about my life and kids. Someone that I don't share as much about is my dad, Dr. John Van Epp. I suppose the reason is that this is a book for moms, and it doesn't have as much of a place for him; however, the framework that this book is built around was developed by him, my dad, in 1980. We have spent over fifteen years working together, and his influence on how I approach relationships, and on this book, is so significant that I would say he is imprinted on just about every page. I've lived and breathed relationships and absorbed his wisdom since I was a young girl. His effect is undeniable, and I'm excited to share one of his greatest gifts to relationship research, literature, and education in this chapter: the Relationship Attachment Model. I am certain that this model will change how you think about relationships forever, including your relationship with yourself.

Dr. John Van Epp first conceptualized the RAM during his clinical counseling work in Medina, Ohio. He drew it on a piece of scrap paper during a session with a female client. Recently he heard from this client that she still has this piece of paper decades later. His concept prompted him to go on a deep research dive, spending countless hours at the library printing and organizing thousands of research studies on the constructs included in the RAM. I know this to be true because I accompanied him on some of these library trips. You may be too young to remember a time when you had to physically go to the library to find articles and make copies of them or print out microfilms (are you now googling *microfilm*?). Well, I was young, but I was there inserting the little white swipe card into the copier, flipping the pages of books, helping my dad develop his brainchild.

He organized all this research and authored a research paper on the model. He went on to teach the model as an adjunct professor of marriage and family therapy classes. Eventually the RAM became the foundation of his first relationship course for singles, which also became his bestselling book, *How to Avoid Falling in Love with a Jerk*. Today, the RAM is the foundational concept in his six relationship courses, all of which have been empirically validated and taught, in total, to around a million people worldwide. The RAM has been featured in textbooks and peer-reviewed journal articles and researched in my dissertation. The bottom line is this: the RAM is legit and empowers you to think differently about relationships.

## WHAT IS THE RELATIONSHIP ATTACHMENT MODEL?

The RAM is a picture of a relationship and the five bonds that make up a relationship. The five bonds are *know, trust, rely, commit*, and *touch*. If you imagine an equalizer on a stereo, the five bonds can be adjusted on sliders moving up and down. This means that each of these bonds can move independently to differing levels, which will create an experience of closeness or an experience of distance. However, these five bonds also interact with one another, meaning that when one bond is decreased, it will likely and eventually start to pull the others down, and vice versa. When you look at the RAM and the arrangement of all five bonds, it tells a story about the relationship. The configuration is a pictorial representation of what the relationship likely feels like, what the experiences are of people in the relationship, and what vulnerabilities may exist.

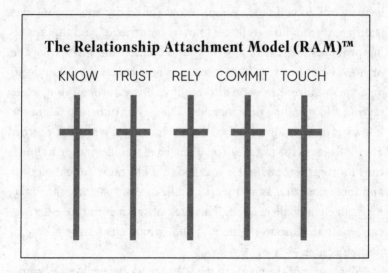

**The Relationship Attachment Model (RAM)™**

KNOW   TRUST   RELY   COMMIT   TOUCH

One of the most powerful aspects of the RAM is that it takes the invisible construct of a relationship, gives it definition, and brings it to life. People tend to say things like "Oh, relationships are so confusing." Yep, that's true, but when you define what a relationship is and what makes up a relationship, it's not as confusing anymore. With the RAM, you can quickly map out your relationship on a model and determine exactly which bonds are suffering and intentionally and strategically make micro-adjustments.

## The Five Relational Bonds

The RAM consists of five relational bonds that exist in *all* relationships. The middle section of this book develops each of these bonds, what they are, and how you can manage them effectively in your relationship with yourself. This section will just provide a brief overview of each of the bonds.

### KNOW

*Know* is how you know others and feel known. When you apply it to yourself, *know* is your insight or self-awareness. There are different degrees of knowing; for example, how you know an acquaintance is different from how well you know a best friend. And this knowing produces feelings of closeness and connection. I'm stating the obvious here, but you feel closer to a best friend than you do to an acquaintance. Knowing also requires effort through things like talking and spending time together. The feeling of being "out of the know" is most easily explained as how it can feel with your partner after kids enter the picture. You likely have trouble finding as much time for togetherness, and if your kids are like mine and talk louder and longer as soon as you start to talk to your partner, then talking is likely a challenge too. This lack of talking and togetherness can lead to a drop in the know bond, which creates the *feeling* of disconnection.

Since none of the bonds of the RAM work independently, knowing informs how you shape your belief (trust) in someone (or yourself) and prompts you to care for others (or yourself) in ways that are meaningful (rely). To love someone (or yourself) in ways that they prefer and desire, you must *know deeply*. More on this in chapter 4.

### TRUST

*Trust* is your belief in someone or confidence in a person that is based on your *opinion about* what you know. When you apply trust to yourself, it is most commonly referred to as your self-concept or self-image. Trust is a powerful construct that has a dramatic influence on how we view others and ourselves. The piece that states opinion about what we know can be tricky, so let me give you an example.

Let's say I have a partner who leaves his discarded socks in piles all around the house on a regular basis. Also, this story is entirely true. That tidbit of information about the socks being left around is what I *factually* know. It's true. Now, my opinion of the socks left around the house is completely in my hands. I get to decide. If my opinion is that leaving socks around the house is something only a selfish person would do, then my trust in (other words: belief in, confidence in, opinion of) my partner would go down. Inevitably, my attitude toward him would likely sour. Now, if my *opinion* of socks left strewn about is that my husband is comfy in our home and he just overlooks things sometimes, then my trust in him (belief, confidence, opinion of) is likely unfazed. I may pick the socks up and roll my eyes because it's too common, I may laugh, or I may nonchalantly say, "Hey, can you grab those socks?" But my attitude toward Chad would not really sour.

I can imagine the pounding of fists: "He should pick up his own stuff—this is part of the problem." I hear you, and I'll leave all commentary on this for my next book! I have two points I want you to take away. First, this example wasn't about socks but rather how our *opinion about* what we factually *know* shapes our trust in others and ourselves. Second, we have control over our opinion and get to decide the narrative that we tell ourselves about what we know. This is why it is so important to *trust accurately* in our relationships with others and ourselves. I will dig into this concept in chapter 5 and how it relates to perfectionism and guilt in motherhood.

## RELY

*Rely* is how you meet the needs of others and they meet your needs. When you apply rely to yourself, it is how you identify, assert, and care for your own needs. Another term would be *self-reliance*.

Meeting the needs of others and having your needs met is bonding. When you give to others, it produces feelings of connection. When others give to you, it does the same. Additionally, when you aren't getting your needs met, disconnection may develop alongside discontentment, resentment, and burnout.

One of the most popular relationship books of all time, *The Five Love Languages* by Gary Chapman, is all about categories of needs in our close romantic relationships. Yet a challenge for so many of us is how to determine what our needs are after we become mothers. The hormonal haze and sleepless nights of those early days and the breakneck speed at which we're thrown into increased responsibilities can make it difficult to adjust our need requests appropriately. We may be shocked and even uncomfortable with how our needs have intensified after having kids. We like to feel independent and self-sufficient, but motherhood turns all these notions on their head. We need others to show up for us, and we need to show up for ourselves. Assuming we can pinpoint our needs, we tend to minimize ourselves for the sake of keeping our relationships running smoothly. In life, and specifically in motherhood, learning how to identify, assert, and care for our needs is paramount. This is why, in chapter 6, I will teach you how to *rely boldly*.

## COMMIT

*Commitment* is the level of investment in a relationship. Commitment alone is bonding. Back in the day when I was younger, we had define-the-relationship talks. Why? Because they spelled out the level of commitment and provided boundaries around the relationship—rules, you could say. They also intensified the connection. Dating was a notch down from being "official," which was a notch down from engaged, and so forth. When you apply commitment to the self, you can think of it as self-regulation and prioritization.

Commitment has three defining aspects: promise, perseverance, and priority. In marriage, promise is the vow you make on your wedding day to stick in the relationship even when it's challenging. We all know the lines "in sickness and in health, for richer or for poorer." This is the promise to persevere even during the hard times, which is the second aspect of commitment. Perseverance is the grit of commitment, which helps you push through a challenging season, work on your marriage when things feel shaky, or get your butt to the gym when you just feel like sleeping in. Commitment also has to do with how we prioritize others in our lives against all the people and things competing for our time and attention.

When it comes to us, a great deal of negative self-talk comes from breaking our promises to ourselves and prioritizing our time and attention in ways that don't always feel good, even if they're necessary. Guilt, shame, and energy depletion are the outcomes of this negative self-talk. This is why we must learn how to *commit wisely*, and I will teach you how to do so in chapter 7.

## TOUCH

*Touch* is bonding and can vary from affectionate words to a high five to loving touch. In our romantic relationships the greatest form of touch is sex. In our relationship with ourselves, touch is best described as self-care. In our closest relationships we don't question the importance of touch. We know it's important in our partnerships, and we experience how much our kids want to touch us, hug us, climb on us, and snuggle us. We intuitively know that this aspect of relationships is absolutely essential. However, the word *self-care* is so played out that we tend to minimize the necessity of touching ourselves in loving ways and listening to our bodies. In chapter 8, I will teach you how to do just that so you can *touch purposefully* in your relationship with yourself.

## PRINCIPLES OF ALL RELATIONSHIPS

At the time of writing this book, Chad and I have been married for fourteen years. In the first five years of marriage, we renovated four homes. The story of each home is a little different, and I'm not going to get into all of that. But what you need to know is that these weren't put-in-new-tile types of renovations; they were "we left one wall to get through permitting" types of renovations—like tearing down the homes and rebuilding on the foundations.

We are not flippers. We built each home with the intention of living in it for years, but life circumstances intervened, and it just didn't work out that way. When we tell people about our renovation-filled relationship, the most common response is "How are you still married?" The truth is, we thrived during renovations. A colleague and friend once gave me an Enneagram guide on relationship pairings. Chad is a 3 and I'm a 9, and it literally said, "You will do well doing something together like renovating homes." Spot on. However, the thriving part of our relationship was one-dimensional. We were like general contractors, talking tile, flooring, and counters and bonding over the irritations of the trades being slow or messing up. What was missing from our relationship was deeper conversation, quality time together, and date nights (who can afford those when you're renovating?). Whenever the flurry of renovating would pass, an adjustment always took place in our relationship. It felt awkward not to be *doing*, and it took time to get comfortable with just *being*. We would have to intentionally create time and space for one another in different ways. We have always recalibrated our connection and closeness after those busy times, but it definitely took effort.

There are three principles that are important to understand in every relationship: life will pull your relationships apart, your relationship does not autocorrect, and you must learn to be an active manager of your relationships.

## Principle 1: Life Will Pull Your Relationship Apart

This sounds dramatic at face value, but we all know it to be true. Life is busy, life is hectic, and life has a way of bringing the unexpected. Or really even the expected. Life is full of responsibilities, interruptions, and obligations that create imbalance in our relationships and disrupt our closeness. This is important to hear: even the good stuff can pull your relationship apart.

Renovating homes was a blessing and thrilling for Chad and me, but it impacted our closeness. Having children is a blessing and thrilling, but it likely impacted your relationship closeness in some way. Becoming a mother is a blessing and thrilling, but I bet it pulled you away from yourself.

Life will mess up our relationships, yet please take comfort because it's totally normal.

This first principle also debunks the myth that balance is possible. I know I said that balance is baloney in the introduction, but it's worth saying again. The goal in relationships is not to find balance. I am not going to teach you how to find balance and stay there forever in motherhood. Why? Because life will mess up your relationship with yourself. Someone will have a sleep regression, you will have to miss work because a kid gets sick, your partner will get laid off, or you will forget that it's teacher appreciation week. There is a momentum to life that naturally pulls us away from connecting in meaningful ways with others and ourselves. Instead, I urge you to embrace the concept of balance-ing—the idea that we, and our relationships, are always fluxing. We are always in motion and changing and dealing with circumstances beyond our control, so we must get comfortable without perfect balance and cozy with the idea that we can make frequent and quick adjustments in how we approach ourselves and our relationships.

**Embrace the concept of balance-ing.**

## Principle 2: Your Relationship Does Not Autocorrect

Just like Chad and I would have to recalibrate our relationship after renovations, you will have to do the same during times of disconnection in your own relationships. If your schedule is unusually busy and you feel like you've had less time to connect with your kids, you'll likely feel less close. You probably don't just let it go; you likely attend to this because you know that it won't fix itself. The same applies to your relationship with yourself: if you feel disconnected from you, maybe you can get by for a bit, but over time this chronic neglect leads to burnout. When your need for rest and respite is greater than any form of self-care can fill, this is because you bought into the idea, whether consciously or unconsciously, that you would just autocorrect. This can be a tough pill to swallow, but I can assure you that you will not autocorrect.

The first principle stated that life will mess us up, it will throw us off-balance, and that is normal. However, chronic imbalances in the five bonds of the RAM will get you into trouble. Whether it's in your relationships with your children or in your relationship with yourself, letting these five levels remain low leaves the relationship vulnerable. In our couple's course, my dad and I share a phrase that says *chronically neglecting these five areas can lead to a flat relationship or a big blowout.* This is no different when applying the RAM to your relationship with yourself. If you chronically neglect these areas, you may become flat—losing yourself in the care for others—or suffer a big blowout—which is burnout—or, worse, physical or mental diagnoses or ailments. I cannot state this strongly enough: your relationships will not autocorrect.

## Principle 3: You Must Learn to Be an Active Manager of Your Relationships

The third principle is a natural response to the first two.

- If life inevitably pulls your relationships apart and

- your relationships do not autocorrect, then
- you must learn to be an active manager of your relationships.

The third principle is sort of laughable when you think about how it applies to you and your relationships with others. Moms are master managers of *all the things* and *all the people*. You do this so well. The challenge of this third principle is learning how to apply your managerial skill set to your relationship with yourself. This brings me back to a line that I will say to you over and over: *you must mother yourself like you mother your kids.* You could substitute *manage* for *mother* in that sentence, but it doesn't sound as warm and inviting. But that is the goal of this book—to teach you how to be so good at managing your relationship with yourself that it becomes second nature, just like it is for how you care for others.

## THE RELATIONSHIP ATTACHMENT MODEL IN ACTION

I am a big believer in the application of concepts to practical scenarios, so I don't want to leave this chapter without helping you see how the RAM provides a picture of what may be going on in your relationships with others and yourself. I am going to apply the RAM to two examples using the same characters—(1) a mother's relationship with her daughter and (2) a mother's relationship with herself—and I will map each on the RAM. Then I would like you to practice doing this for your relationships with each of your children and then finally your relationship with yourself.

In case any of you are overthinkers, I want to clear something up. The way you arrange each of the five dynamics on the RAM can change day to day or even moment to moment. So how you complete these pictures is based on whatever is going on for you at this exact time and doesn't need to capture the "average" of your relationship functioning or how you do over time. Just consider where you would fall on each of the dynamics in this moment in time.

## Scenario 1: Christy's Relationship with Mia

Christy is a thirty-two-year-old mom to Mia (three years old). She is currently a stay-at-home mom after leaving her job when Mia was born. Mia is what some would call a deeply feeling child; in other words, she feels things in really big ways. She has throw-down tantrums two or three times a day, and Christy has started to avoid leaving the house for fear of having to deal with one in a public place. Mia isn't very verbal, and Christy has a hard time figuring out what is setting off Mia's tantrums. Christy usually ends up exasperated and frustrated by the end of a tantrum and finds herself losing her cool more than she wants. The cumulative effect of the tantrums and the intensity of emotions coming from Mia has impacted Christy's opinion of her, and she's noticed that she has started labeling her daughter, out loud sometimes, as dramatic and difficult. Otherwise, Christy and Mia have a good relationship. Mia wants to be held a lot, and they have lots of fun playing with bubbles and reading books.

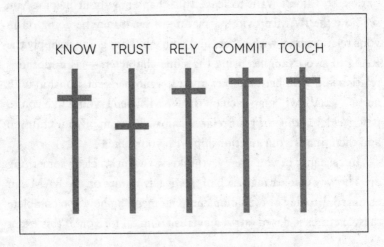

KNOW   TRUST   RELY   COMMIT   TOUCH

## EXPLAINING THE LEVELS

1. KNOW: Know is slightly down, primarily because Mia is not able to communicate what she needs to Christy. One likely reason for Mia's tantrums is that she experiences frustration over not being able to communicate effectively. But this lack of knowledge makes this part of their relationship challenging for Christy, and she's forced to intuit things based on what she does know about Mia.

2. TRUST: Trust is also down because Christy's opinion of Mia is starting to shift. She factually knows that Mia has tantrums, and this has translated into a belief that Mia is dramatic and difficult. Likely, this negative belief or trust picture (more in chapter 5) is translating into a negative attitude toward Mia. It's possible that this belief accelerates Christy's frustration because each meltdown reinforces the idea that "I have a difficult and dramatic daughter."

3. RELY: Rely is down just slightly. Christy is trying to meet Mia's needs. She desperately wants to help, but her lack of knowing (among other things) can make this challenging.

4. COMMIT: Commitment is still high. Christy is prioritizing Mia, and the commitment between a mother and a child is often at the highest level.

5. TOUCH: Touch is also high. Christy works to reconnect with Mia after the tantrums and holds her when she finally calms down. Christy holds Mia often, and they have lots of fun together, playing and reading on the couch with Mia in her lap.

## SUMMARY

You can see from the configuration on the RAM places of possible intervention. The middle section of the book describes each of the five dynamics in depth, so I'm not going to hash this out; however, one targeted way to recalibrate the relationship would be to have Christy work on challenging her opinion, or her trust picture (more in chapter 5), of Mia. If she changed her opinion of Mia as "dramatic and difficult" to "my child is having a hard time," this would likely alter the way she felt during the tantrums and how she responded to Mia and ultimately would result in her losing her cool less often.

## Scenario 2: Christy's Relationship with Herself

Christy loves being a stay-at-home mom, but she's felt worn down from managing all Mia's big feelings throughout the day. She finds herself fantasizing about going back to work. She has noticed that she is losing her cool more with Mia and then feels guilty and ashamed for some of the ways she acts and things she says. Mia seems to be in the midst of a sleep regression, and Christy's partner works nights and sleeps during the day, so she isn't getting the rest she needs or support during the day so she can have a break. She feels worn down, exhausted, and grumpy. She hates feeling this way and assumes this is a phase that will pass.

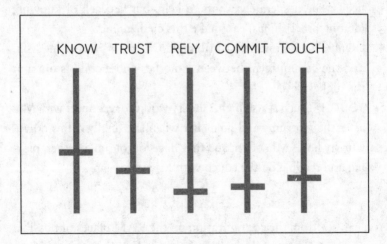

KNOW   TRUST   RELY   COMMIT   TOUCH

EXPLAINING THE LEVELS

1. KNOW: Know is down. Christy feels out of touch with her former self. She has loved being at home with Mia but also can

experience feelings of sadness about not having her work identity anymore. Since she spends much of the day just surviving, it can feel like what she does all day doesn't have a lot of meaning. She also hates that she loses it sometimes. This feels out of character, and she sometimes doesn't recognize herself.

2. TRUST: Trust is down. Christy's opinion of herself has really suffered. She feels guilty most of the time for either not keeping her cool or for having to leave the room when Mia has a meltdown. She replays the narrative "a good mom wouldn't react this way" over and over in her head, and it has worn her out.

3. RELY: Rely is down. Christy doesn't have much support and is unable to find the time and space to care for her needs. She doesn't feel comfortable asking her partner for help since he works such long hours, and because she's a stay-at-home mom, she feels like she "shouldn't" need the time. She's conflicted; she knows she needs to speak up, but she also feels too guilty to ask. She can't seem to find the courage, and her needs are being neglected because of it.

4. COMMIT: Commit is also down. Christy has been unable to prioritize herself. She also has run out of capacity to self-regulate, and her willpower is at an all-time low (more in chapter 8).

5. TOUCH: Touch is down. Christy's physical self is speaking, and it's telling her, "You're tired; you need support." She feels stressed, isn't sleeping, and overall is run ragged. She's also isolated because she hasn't felt comfortable leaving the house with Mia, and her partner is either gone or sleeping much of the time.

## SUMMARY

Christy is suffering. Her configuration on the RAM represents many of us moms. Our relationships with our kids or our partners may look much better, but our foundational relationship with ourselves is in shambles. These two configurations are not independent. If Christy were able to tackle even one area on the RAM, the other bonds would be positively impacted, and this would eventually alter her relationship with Mia. This point is a powerful one: *when you care for yourself in meaningful ways, your relationships will naturally shift, even if the other person does nothing differently.* You have personal power to make changes. If Christy couldn't find time for physical care for herself but could work to shift her attitude toward herself, no doubt she would have more capacity to keep it together in tough moments with Mia. Why? Well, you'll learn more in chapters 5 and 8, but negative self-talk drains willpower. And when you have less willpower, you lose it more, and that feeds negative self-talk. There are many areas in which Christy could make micro-adjustments, and those will be explored more deeply later in the book.

## Your Turn

Now I'd like for you to chart out your relationship with each of your kids and then with yourself. Remember, this is just a reflection of where your relationships are right at this very moment; these could change in the next hour or week. If this feels difficult, please take heart that there is no wrong way of doing this. You can't chart out your relationship incorrectly; this is just an exercise to help you apply the RAM to your real life. It will help bring the concepts to life as you move through the rest of the chapters. No pressure to be perfect—just do it! This exercise will help you to visualize where your relationships with your kids and your relationship with yourself may need some attention. It is also powerful in that it will

start to give definition to your experience. If you feel burned-out but don't know why, you'll likely start to understand more after mapping out your relationship with yourself. Scan the QR code for downloadable RAM worksheets that you can revisit whenever you need to.

## PROMISE OF THIS BOOK

The RAM is your self-management model, and what you manage are the five bonds that compose the RAM. The RAM is your plan, and the bonds are the five steps you will review each time you check in on your relationship with yourself. Because it's a picture, you will remember it and be able to take it with you in all your relationships. Within the RAM are both simplicity and complexity: simplicity because it's easy to use and remember and complexity because each of the five dynamics unpacks deep and meaningful concepts like insight, self-awareness, guilt, perfectionism, attachment styles, will-power, stress, and so on.

My hope for you is that you will embrace your role as a self-manager because you're important and necessary to the health and vitality of your family and society as a whole. I hope you embrace caring for you on a deep level because you are important—period, end of statement.

My other hope for you is that you find that this model and these concepts equip and empower you with practical ways to make micro-adjustments in how you relate to yourself. I hope that you regularly practice checking in with you, but instead of just realizing you're burned-out, you feel you have the know-how to do something about it. Or, if nothing else, you have definition to what you are experiencing, and that definition offers some feeling of control and liberation.

In the sections that follow, I will take you through each of the five bonds, and these will become your five steps for self-check-ins.

Step 1: Know deeply
Step 2: Trust accurately
Step 3: Rely boldly
Step 4: Commit wisely
Step 5: Touch purposefully

The chapters are structured such that first you will go deep into the psychological concepts and constructs held within each area of the RAM, and then I will move into the practical application of each to your life. I will give you the tools to accomplish these steps.

There may be times that the deep information feels overwhelming, but I assure you that the understanding of these concepts will radically shift how you relate to yourself and others. The deep stuff isn't something you will remain permanently entrenched in either. The goal is for you to have a good understanding of the concepts and then be able to quickly access the skills moving forward. Journey one time through the deep waters, and then just dip your toes into the skills as needed as you make micro-adjustments in your relationship with yourself.

To be clear, once you have these concepts down, your self-check-in can be done quickly. I am a mom too; I know the importance of time and how it feels like there's never enough. Please know that your check-in may be done in the same amount of time it takes to go on a quick trip to the bathroom. Instead of scrolling while sitting on the toilet, you check in with you. You run through the five steps, determine where your deficits are, and decide what you can do about them at this time. Sometimes this will mean shifting your thoughts; sometimes it will be something bigger. Either way, you will have all the information to *know* what you need to adjust and *how* to make that adjustment.

There may be times during your life when big shifts occur that prompt you to revisit the deeper concepts. These concepts are tried-and-true and will relate to your life no matter the stage you're in or the age of your children. Refresh as needed.

I can appreciate how little time we moms have. At the end of each chapter, I have a section called "Go Mom Yourself," which is a shorter and punchier way of saying mother yourself like you mother your kids. It contains a summary of each of the steps. This can be your quick reference guide, should you need help remembering the skills reviewed in the chapters.

*part two*

# five steps for
# transformation

# *Chapter Four*

## STEP 1: KNOW DEEPLY

The other day my husband, Chad, gave the kids a bath. I was making dinner upstairs in the kitchen when I heard the kids shrieking. I ran downstairs, unaware of what I was going to walk into. Were they bleeding out? Did I leave my razor in the tub or something? Should I grab a first aid kit on the way? Call 911? It's wild how after becoming moms we have the enhanced ability to imagine thousands of deadly situations we must protect our kids from. This leads me to the overarching question that was playing through my mind: *What the heck was my husband doing to take care of this potential life-or-death situation?*

I walked into the bathroom to find Roy standing up, screaming, and grabbing his bum. My husband looked at me with bewilderment—you know the look. It's the look that says we, the moms, have all the answers. "Roy said his butt feels spicy."

Effie, who was taking a shower, cracked open the door and yelled, "Dad used the peppermint soap on him; he should have known better." She then shut the glass door and shook her head in utter annoyance.

This story isn't meant to pick on my husband, or on all husbands and dads for that matter. I've got a good one who is always willing to jump in and share the load. But the fact remains that my husband didn't know our kids don't use peppermint soap despite the fact that he's been a father for the last eight years. Maybe he didn't know because he doesn't give them baths enough, or maybe he didn't know because his job requires a lot of travel, so I do most of the day-to-day stuff with the kids. Either way, there are often gaps in how well we know our kids, and their experiences can easily get overlooked or missed.

## KNOWING AS AN ACT OF LOVE

In order to care for our kids in the ways they prefer and need, we must know them. My husband didn't know this minor detail about our kids, and Roy's butt paid the price. When we know our kids well, we're then able to care for them and love them in the ways they need. The same goes for all our relationships.

I see this come up all the time when I talk about the mental load or invisible labor of motherhood. One of the most common reactions moms have is "It's easier to just do it myself." Why is that? It's easier because we *know* what to do, *how* to do it, how all the people in our families *like* it, and *where* all of it is. Moms are experts of knowing, which is one of the reasons we're so incredible at intuiting and initiating caretaking of our kids and families.

The bottom line is this: to care for and love others well, you must know them deeply. The same notion applies to you. To care for and love yourself well, you must know yourself deeply. When you know yourself and others deeply, you gain an understanding of why you are the way you are, what triggers you have, why you perceive things in certain ways, and what needs you have.

Knowing goes beyond just understanding someone's preferences for soap or the way your kids like their bread sliced. Knowing is bonding. Knowing forges feelings of safety, connection, and closeness. Knowing requires caring enough to be curious, paying enough attention to observe another's world, and striving to obtain the exclusive information that only insiders are privy to. To be fully known and still loved? Well, that's the jackpot!

Knowing our children well is one of the greatest privileges of motherhood. I think this is one of the reasons many young kids have a preference for their moms. We usually know them the best, and feeling known elicits a sense of safety and connection.

Conversely, being "out of the know" feels like disconnection and distance. I have no doubt there are times when you've been away from your kids—whether it's because you're working, they're at school, you've taken a trip, or you just had a few hours apart—and you come back together with a sense of being out of tune.

Being "in the know" or "out of the know" has a dramatic impact on the closeness in your relationship with your kids. The same applies for your relationship with yourself.

This chapter is about knowing deeply. It's the why, the what, and the how of knowing yourself and your kids. After reading it, you'll better understand why what you don't know can unintentionally harm you or your relationships, how knowledge is powerful because it puts you in the driver's seat of your relationships, and how knowing your kids and yourself is ongoing because knowledge doesn't have an endpoint, and life inevitably gets busy and promotes disconnection.

## WHAT YOU DON'T KNOW CAN HURT YOU (OR OTHERS)

Knowing has different depths. When we're asked, "Hey, do you know Alex?" you may say, "Yes, we're best friends," which indicates you know one another well. Or you may say, "Yes, she's an acquaintance," which suggests a surface level of relationship.

We refer to depths of knowing people without really thinking about it. It's just part of our common nomenclature.

I think of the depths of knowing through the imagery of the ocean. On the surface we see waves. If we know nothing more about the ocean than the presence of waves, we can make up reasons for why they exist. Maybe it's the wind? Maybe it's an earthquake? With only primitive knowledge of the ocean, we're left with no other information than what we see on the surface.

Now, if we have a deeper sense of knowing, we go below the surface. We see that the ocean floor impacts the patterns and appearance of waves. To someone with limited knowledge, a wave is just a wave. To someone with deeper knowing, these waves take on all sorts of different shapes and meanings depending on what's going on below the surface.

Then there are the depths of the ocean that largely remain unexplored and unknown to the average person. However, expert oceanographers are dedicated to understanding the oceans and all their wonder. They go deep below the surface waters. Going this deep requires effort, commitment, and motivation. Not just anyone can easily acquire the knowledge of these depths of the ocean; there must be a desire to know and a commitment to pursue this knowledge.

When Roy was four, I got a call from the director of the preschool he attended. She requested that I come in that day and have a meeting with her and Roy's teacher. I rearranged my schedule and hustled down the road and up the hill to the preschool parking lot I'd parked in hundreds of times. I took a massive deep breath, attempting to gather myself before walking into the conference room. I had no idea what to expect and was feeling anxious because of the sense of urgency in the director's voice.

Upon entering the office, I sat down on those itchy chairs that so often fill administrative offices and greeted them both. The director started by telling me how Roy had hit another student in the head with a block the day before.

Yikes. That wasn't good.

The director continued to explain how she and Roy's teacher were concerned that he mostly played alone, didn't talk much, and was violent toward the other student.

I sat silently, trying to regulate my surging mix of humiliation and defensiveness.

The director continued speaking, suggesting that I teach Roy to articulate his feelings.

*Duh*, I thought to myself. I wondered, *Is this my chance to throw my degree around? Or does that just make me look incompetent? A relationship expert with a PhD sucks at parenting but is great at raising a sociopath! Nah, I'll just listen.*

"Maybe you're watching too many violent shows at home?" she wondered out loud. "I know how he likes superheroes."

That was it. I'd had enough. I knew that Roy had been labeled based on their surface knowledge of him. These two saw Roy's waves and drew their own conclusions. They weren't curious about what lurked underneath. It was my turn to talk.

I apologized for his behavior and reassured them both that I would continue to talk with Roy about how to manage big feelings.

"I do have a question though," I continued. "Have you ever noticed that Roy curls up in a tiny ball during the day?"

"Yes!" his teacher exclaimed. "I just never really thought much about it."

*Yeah, no kidding*, I thought.

"Roy has done this ever since he was little. He does it when he is really upset and feels unsafe or ashamed. It's his way of trying to regulate. He pulls his whole body in, and then he doesn't act out his big feelings. I didn't teach him this. It's just something he's done since he could move on his own.

"I think you should also know how Roy talks about school," I continued. "He's a highly sensitive kid and an excellent storyteller, so I know there's often some artistic embellishment to his tales. But daily, he has stories about being chased, bullied, or messed with at school. I am not sure of the specifics, but I am sure of the theme: he doesn't feel safe.

"I also can recall the day he hit the other child with the block, and I suspect I know which child he hit. Every day at drop-off, I hang around until Roy feels settled. I'm sure you've noticed," I said, looking at his teacher. "We almost always build something together. At some point, Roy lets me know when he's good, and that's when I leave. It takes him time to feel comfortable. That day, we built a large tower. As we were building, another boy kept threatening to knock Roy's tower down. We both asked him politely not to touch it. I'm just wondering—did Roy's tower get knocked down before he hit the boy with the block?"

"Yes!" said his teacher. This detail was nowhere to be found in the original telling of the incident.

"Okay," I said. "This makes more sense to me. I'm not excusing Roy's behavior, and we will talk about this in great depth. However, I don't think you're interpreting him correctly. He's nervous and has a great deal of anxiety at school, and I think he's being labeled as a bad kid. I think that this impacts how you see him and possibly manage him during the day."

The director of the preschool chimed in, "It's so clear to me now, Morgan. I'm so sorry we missed this. I think I know exactly what to do. What do you think about moving Roy into a smaller class? It has only eight kids."

When I checked in with the director after a trial week in the new class, she couldn't believe how much Roy talked. "He's telling me all sorts of stories! He's like an entirely new kid."

Except Roy was the *same* kid. He was just known on a deeper level, seen more accurately, and taken care of in the way he needed.

That's what knowing deeply promotes: connection, accurate

perceptions, and the ability to meet needs in the ways that are most important and meaningful.

Roy's preschool experience changed after that meeting. He blossomed. For a moment, imagine if my knowledge of Roy was shallow. What if I only looked at his waves? How would I have cared for him and represented him differently during that encounter with his teacher and the preschool director? Imagine if my worth as a mother was tethered to his behavior. How might I have reacted differently? How might I have talked to Roy later on about my meeting with his teacher and the director?

When we don't take a deeper look at what impacts our waves or our children's, we cannot love them and care for them in the ways they need. Instead, we may react harshly or impulsively, draw inaccurate conclusions, or not love our kids or ourselves in the ways we need the most.

This concept may stir up anxiety in you. *What if I think I'm in the deep blue waters—only to learn I'm in the waves? This just adds to the pressure that I may mess up my kid.*

I get it. And let me reassure you—we will miss things. Sometimes we'll use peppermint soap, misunderstand something, or be too busy to do a deep dive into our children's behavior. It's okay. Our interactions and the quality of relationships with our kids aren't determined by a singular moment but by the totality of our experiences together. There's room to get it wrong sometimes and still have a close and connected relationship.

We all have things lurking below our waves that we must explore because these things impact us—how we behave, what triggers us, how we feel, and how we perceive the world around us. We have to do a deep dive in order to know both our kids and ourselves well. Otherwise, we're just reacting to, and

> **There's room to get it wrong sometimes and still have a close and connected relationship.**

being impacted by, our circumstances or experiences without deeper examination. When we do this, what we don't know can hurt us and others.

Knowing deeply requires unearthing the roots of who you are and examining them so you can care for and love yourself more fully. It's self-awareness. It's seeing yourself honestly so you can make conscious decisions to either repeat the patterns of your past or create new ones.

## KNOWLEDGE IS POWER

Without self-awareness, you are almost certain to repeat patterns from your past. Oftentimes this pattern operates outside your awareness and will end up, unfortunately, reinforcing itself. Freud called this "repetition compulsion." Repetition compulsion is a psychological phenomenon where someone is believed to reenact life events or situations in an attempt to change the ending.[1] Think of a friend who continues to choose horrible partners who all closely resemble the relationship she had with her father.

Freud believed one of the main tenets in disrupting repetition compulsion was insight. He found that consciously identifying the reason for a behavior offered the ability to do something with it. Information and insight are empowering because when we have them, we can make conscious decisions. We can hold that information up, examine it, and ask ourselves, *Does this still work for me? Does this fit my reality? Does this serve me?* Then, most importantly, we can choose what we want to do with it. Insight is the starting point for powerful changes.

Let me give you an example of how repetition compulsion can operate.

Meet Jessie. Growing up, Jessie was regularly told that she was dramatic. Her parents reminded her often that she could be defensive, loud, and full of big feelings. While her parents had good intentions, they were unaware of the messaging received by Jessie: "Settle down. Calm down. Go to your room. This is too much for us." These were the messages she internalized from her parents. So, over the years, Jessie learned to cope by stuffing her big feelings. She knew that her parents loved her most when she was easiest for them, so she tried to be as easy as possible.

Fast-forward to Jessie's adulthood, in which she is now a mom. She has a young daughter with some majorly big feelings. She's really triggered by her daughter's meltdowns and finds that she, in turn, can't handle them. Jessie feels completely out of control, like she's failing at motherhood. Her heart races, she rages inside, and she leaves. She retreats to her room, locking the door in an attempt to calm down, trying to muffle the wailing of her kid in the distance.

Jessie isn't a bad mom—not by any stretch of the imagination. However, she is influenced by her past in a way that's creeping into her present. She feels dysregulated when her child becomes dysregulated. She was taught at an early age to stuff her emotions so she wasn't unruly or dramatic. Now, when big feelings approach in adulthood, she's reminded of this messaging. She stuffs her feelings down, and when she can't, it overwhelms her. An important piece to Jessie's story is that she's responding to her child in a way that conveys the same message she received: "You're too much when you feel big things." This sets the stage for her future relationship with her daughter and how she will ultimately handle her emotions.

If Jessie knew herself deeply, she'd know where her big reactions to her daughter's tantrums come from. She could then depersonalize the meaning of those reactions, such as remembering that her emotional response isn't a reflection of her merit as a mom. Then she could consciously choose a new path forward by disrupting the pattern of her own experiences. This would heal her heart and protect her daughter's heart simultaneously. This is a perfect example of the mutually beneficial exchanges in motherhood I referred to in chapter 2.

Knowledge is power. Knowing yourself deeply allows you to decide intentionally if you want to repeat patterns in your life.

The idea that we're influenced by our past isn't a new one. It's important to know that pieces of our past can sometimes lie dormant for years, like seeds taking root below the surface. Motherhood and the challenges of raising kids often provide the water and sunshine needed for those seeds to grow and blossom. In motherhood, feelings may arise that you didn't experience before, but I'd wager these feelings aren't really that new. They were just hidden, existing under the surface, waiting for the right conditions to grow.

## Knowing Your Past

Digging deep into your past can take thousands of dollars and years in therapy, but I want to walk you through three targeted areas of your past, along with questions for connecting your past to your present. Then I'll give you three things to consider as you care for yourself and raise your children.

There are three main areas to explore when knowing yourself deeply, all of which are related to your early experiences with your caregivers: how love was shown, how emotions were expressed, and how you formed your identity and expectations.

As you work through this section of the chapter, it can be helpful to use a journal or diary to make notes. Please note that there are all sorts of families, all of which come with different histories and experiences. Your main caregivers may have been your mom and dad, a single mom, a single dad, a foster family, adoptive parents, and so on. There are endless combinations of families. If you had numerous main caregivers, you may have to explore each of these relationships. Please approach this section with self-compassion.

## 1. HOW LOVE WAS SHOWN

The first area to explore is how your main caregivers showed you love. You can think of love on a continuum. On one end is the cold and distant family: this family doesn't say "I love you," and they probably don't express or show much affection to one another. In this family, you may have just assumed you were loved, not because anyone said it, but because that's what families are supposed to feel for one another.

On the other end of the continuum is the gregarious, highly affectionate family: this family likely lays it on thick. They may hug and kiss a lot and easily throw around "I love you."

Understanding how you were shown love is important because we're wired for relationships. When we don't receive the love we need, we're highly motivated to adapt in ways that maximize connection. You may explore these questions and realize you've made concessions or modifications throughout your life to get the love you desire. Or maybe you avoid uncomfortable feelings around love and expression. As you consider these questions, pay particular attention to how your early experiences impact you today:

- How did you know you were loved?
- How did you see others in your home express love to one another?
- Were there any conditions to receiving love in your home?
- When did you feel like your caregivers loved you the most?

## 2. HOW EMOTIONS WERE EXPRESSED

Emotions, like love, can be thought of on a continuum. You can think of the expressions of emotion on a scale of closed to open.

On the closed end would be a family that is relatively flat. Not much emotion is expressed in the home, and too much emotion is likely viewed as a problem.

LOVE YOUR KIDS WITHOUT LOSING YOURSELF

If you get emotional in this family, you're perceived as overreacting, dramatic, or sensitive. You may be asked, "Why are you acting like such a baby? What's the big deal?" Not a lot of attention is paid to emotional needs in a home like this. Family mantras are something like "Control the controllables" or "There's no use in getting upset." It's important to note that these statements, made occasionally, are okay. There is wisdom to only worrying about what you can control. But when the rule, rather than the exception, of the family is that emotions are bad, then your experience may be somewhere on the extreme of the closed end of the spectrum.

On the other extreme, the open end of the spectrum, is a family with no boundaries for emotions. This type of family may exhibit major emotional swings or outbursts. These families may have trouble self-regulating, or they may express their emotions in hurtful ways.

It's likely your caregivers and home environment were somewhere in between the two extremes. It's important to explore this area because it has a major impact on how you understand, react to, interpret, and express your emotions in your adult life.

Consider the following questions:

- When I was upset (i.e., angry, hurt, or sad) as a kid, how did my caregivers respond to me?
- What messages did I receive from my caregivers about my emotions?
- What skills were modeled or taught for regulating emotions?
- How did I see my caregivers express emotions?
- How did my caregivers regulate their own emotions?

### 3. HOW YOU FORMED YOUR IDENTITY AND EXPECTATIONS

I grew up with a mom who was incredibly nurturing. She was a stay-at-home mom for the majority of my life and dedicated herself to raising my sister and me and to caring for our home and her husband. My parents were quite traditional. This was the maternal model I witnessed growing up.

When Chad and I first got married, we lived in a townhouse in Fairfax, Virginia. The floor plan was open, and when I was cooking, I could see right into the living room. I have vivid memories of making dinner in the kitchen and then reassuring Chad that I would also take care of the dishes. "Don't worry, babe. I've got this," I'd say night after night.

Chad, at first, put up a fight. Eventually, he capitulated and found a good resting spot for his butt on the couch. I washed the dishes cheerfully—for a while.

Over time I found myself creating a bit more noise in the kitchen, occasionally banging a pot or a pan like a cowbell in an attempt to call him to take over the cleaning duties. After all, I'd thought of the meal, shopped for the food, and cooked it. Why was I now cleaning it too? I was starting to build resentment and frustration.

The ridiculous part is that my husband was always willing to do the job. I'd just fired him.

I took on the role of doing all the things early on in our marriage because that's what I saw my mother do growing up. My early experiences formed expectations for the role and identity I'd take on in my future family.

I didn't even think about it; it was automatic. The dormant seeds of expectation simply require the right conditions to bloom and grow. And marriage tends to facilitate the first round of growth, followed by parenthood. In marriage, I fell into the role of the nurturing and caretaking wife—even at the expense of my own desires and needs.

I had to identify this tendency and then intentionally choose to change course. I worked and was in school. My mom's demands had been different. I couldn't do all the things without developing resentment, but maybe my mom could (although I remember her angrily vacuuming the garage because "no one else would").

I would bet you can identify a similar experience in your own life, like that moment when you catch yourself cleaning up for the cleaning lady just like your mom did. Or maybe you realize you've set the bar so high for motherhood because you idealized your own mother. Our relationship with our caregiver of the same sex forms our expectations of the role that we fulfill in the family we create and the identity we take on as a woman, wife, and mother.

These expectations don't necessarily mean that you'll become a carbon copy of your same-sex caregiver, but your relationship with this caregiver is majorly influential. When you finally unearth these influences (meaning, gain that insight), you may realize, much like I did, that they don't work for you, and you may need to make adjustments. That's the power of knowing. When you know the issue, you have the agency to do something different with it.

Our relationship with our caregiver of the opposite sex is also important to explore. This forms our expectations of what we want a partner to be like in the family we create, both as a partner and a parent. This also affects how we perceive and define masculinity. Unmet expectations are often a massive source of disappointment and resentment in relationships, especially in a relationship with a partner. Unearth these expectations by exploring your relationship with the opposite-sex caregiver. You can't explain your expectations, or even examine them, if they remain deep below the surface.

Consider the following questions:

- What was my relationship like with my parent of the same sex?
- What was my relationship like with my parent of the opposite sex?
- If your mother was married, what was she like as a wife?
- How was I mothered? What did this teach me? What stuck with me?

- What expectations do I have for myself as a mother?
- What expectations do I have for my partner as a parent? As a partner?

## Looking to the Future

As you have uncovered different insights and realizations about your early experiences, it can feel enlightening but also disheartening. Now, what do you do with this information?

This is one of the most brilliant parts of adulthood: you have the autonomy to choose a new way forward! You didn't get to choose the family you grew up in, but you get to choose the type of family you create.

My mother was adopted at two months old. She was first given up by her biological mother and next placed with a family that treated her like they didn't want her either. Her past experiences became her fire for future change. She knew what it felt like to be alone, rejected, and not nurtured—and she was determined to shape her children's future differently. Her hurts were my sister's and my gain. She made meaning from her painful experiences and willfully chose to do things differently.

You can do the same. Painful life experiences are often the breeding ground for profound growth and change. You don't need pain to grow, but if you've experienced it, know that it doesn't have to go to waste. You, too, can make meaning of your hurts and use them to cultivate a different relationship with your kids.

After you've had time to reflect on the previous questions, outline these three areas to help organize the changes you'd like to implement in your life and in your relationships with your kids.

Reflect on your growing-up experience, and ask yourself:

1. What do I want to make sure I repeat with my children?
2. What would I like to add that wasn't a part of my growing-up experience?

3. What do I want to make sure I don't repeat in my relationships with my children?

Phew! You survived the deep-dive portion of this chapter. The questions in this section may be ones that you work through and never have to return to again. They may lead to aha moments that require more work on your end. They also may be questions that stir things up and prompt you to go to counseling or talk more deeply with others in your life.

You may want to periodically return to these questions to check yourself. They can serve as a guide to see how you're aligning with the goals you want in the family you create. You can also use them to check your current reactions and perceptions against your early formative experiences.

No matter how they impacted you, these questions are designed to help you gain insight into who you are, why you are the way you are, and why you may have the expectations, triggers, and world-view you do. These questions are intended to help you understand your foundational and unchanging past experiences.

## KNOWING IS ONGOING

What you know one day may or may not be true the next. We're ever-changing beings, just like our kids. One day they want their bread sliced horizontally, while the next day they'll want it diagonally. They're moving targets—and so are we. Knowing our kids, and ourselves, deeply isn't a final destination. Knowing is ongoing.

Life gets busy, and it demands ebb and flow. We occasionally sacrifice staying in tune with our kids and ourselves just to make it through the day. After all, there's not always as much time as we'd like for touching base with one another.

I have no doubt that there are times when you've been away

from your kids only to come back together with a sense of being out of touch with each other. To reconnect, you probably initiate a hug, a conversation, or special time together. Falling out of touch with our kids happens with no effort, yet getting back in touch takes some intention.

This same concept applies to how we relate to ourselves. Falling out of the know with ourselves takes no effort, yet getting back in the know also requires intention. You've probably had a moment, or many moments, when you've looked in the mirror and wondered, *Who the heck is this woman staring back at me? I don't even recognize myself anymore.* This is normal and likely more intense at different stages of motherhood, but this isn't a sustainable way of life.

If you become disconnected from your kids and remain that way, your relationship with them will undoubtedly be affected. If you are disconnected from yourself and remain that way for the majority of motherhood, you run the risk of experiencing that deep, soul-crushing emptiness when your children are grown. You run the risk of being the mother who just can't seem to let her kids go—because if you aren't their mother and aren't needed by them, then who are you anyway?

When it comes to your kids, I'm sure you know exactly how to get back in the know. You likely sit down and talk with them, do something together, or increase the amount of time you're with them. Yet when we feel out of the know with ourselves, the answer isn't always so clear.

## STAYING IN THE KNOW WITH YOURSELF

We tend to feel "not like ourselves" when we're incongruent. When we're distant from the person we perceive ourselves to be, it's easy to feel out of the know. Let me give you some examples of what this can look like:

- When you know yourself as someone who's controlled yet you can't keep your cool when your kid throws tantrums, you'll feel disconnected from who you know yourself to be.
- When you know you're someone who derives purpose from accomplishments at work but you're on maternity leave, you may not feel like yourself.
- When you know yourself as someone who values productivity yet you can't get a darn thing done with your kids around, you'll likely feel frustrated and not like your whole self.

When you feel disconnected from yourself and out of the know, look for the incongruencies in your life. In particular, examine the following three areas that form the acronym MIA (in hopes of helping you recall these easily):

- MEANING: *I live my life in a way that feels meaningful* versus *I am not currently living in a way that feels meaningful.*
- IMPORTANCE: *I am living out things that are important to me* versus *I am not living out things that are important to me.*
- ALIGNMENT: *I am living in a way that is consistent with how I see myself* versus *I am living in a way that doesn't feel like the me that I know.*

The first time I flew alone after having kids was when our oldest was five years old. Five years—do you hear me? Five years of boarding a plane like a pack mule. Five years of carrying on a backpack full of diapers, snacks, and toys. I was pumped, to put it lightly. I got to exist for a short amount of time as a singular person, only in charge of myself, my needs, my time frame. Just me. It was glorious.

Part of what made this trip so special was that I was going to a conference as a keynote speaker. Not only did I get to have one night—twenty-four full, sweet hours to myself—but I also got to feel important for things beyond making dinner and doing a good Doc McStuffins impression.

I walked into the conference feeling really good. I saw someone I hadn't seen since having our two kids, and she gave me a big hug and said, "Morgan! Morgan! Oh my goodness, look at you! You're such a mom."

What the heck?!

I am not sure what I did in that moment, but I probably just smiled. What's so crazy is that she later ran up to me for the express purpose of saying it again. "Morgan! You look beautiful, but you're just such a mom now."

The reason this well-intentioned woman's words hit me so hard was because, for the first time in five years, I truly felt like my former self. I felt aligned and put together, something I hadn't felt since becoming a mom. I felt congruent with what gives me meaning: teaching others about relationships. I was doing something important to me by speaking at a conference that I used to be a mainstay at. I was harmonious with the Morgan I was before becoming a mom, and it felt so good.

But I couldn't live in that world, at least not permanently. Still, I hadn't fully adapted to my current world with the Morgan who drops the ball, who's rushing more than she likes, who isn't always dressed, and who struggles to have the amount of time she wants to devote to her work.

To get back "in the know" with me, I had to revisit the three categories of incongruencies—meaning, importance, and alignment—and make adjustments.

I had to shift my self-perception and identity (more on this in chapter 5) to fit my new role as a mom, particularly as a stay-at-home working mom. I had to reevaluate what is important to me. And I had to assess where I really derive my meaning from. I also needed to expand what gave me a sense of meaning to incorporate how I felt about my role as a mother. Finally, I had to make adjustments (more on this in chapter 7) to maximize and prioritize what brought my life meaning.

Use these three touch points as a guided reflection when you feel out of touch with yourself. Examine your own incongruencies. Then make the adjustments as necessary.

Ask yourself:

- MEANING: Am I living in a way that feels meaningful to me?
- IMPORTANCE: Am I living out things that are important to me?
- ALIGNMENT: Am I living in a way that is consistent with how I see myself?

If you aren't sure how you see yourself, what's important to you, or what brings your life meaning, check out the activity in the "A Deeper Dive" section of the book.

## ANCHORING TO YOUR TRUE SELF WHEN ALL ELSE IS INCONGRUENT

When it comes to knowing deeply, there tend to be truths, or anchors, that tether us to our true selves. These anchors remain relatively stable and secure, either through our lives or through seasons of life.

Take, for example, the time I was at a park with one of my close friends. We were talking about the different seasons of motherhood. She said that when she first became a mother, she decided one of the most important messages she wanted to convey to her children was that she genuinely wanted to be with them. She wanted them to know she enjoys them and wants to be in their presence. This served as her anchor.

Even when she was feeling incongruent, adjusting to her many identity shifts throughout motherhood, or when she felt like her meaning and purpose were on the back burner, she could return to that anchor. "As long as I am a mother who conveys to my kids how much I want them in my life, I feel like myself." That truth was steady and helped her feel like her true self.

You can work on developing your own anchor for when you feel "out of the know" with yourself (see activity in "A Deeper Dive"). This can be your "quick grab" technique to feel congruent and like you're thinking, feeling, or behaving in a way that's representative of who you know yourself to be. When you're able to do this, you'll feel that you are known deeply and in touch with yourself.

## *Go Mom Yourself*

### Step 1: Know Deeply

- Examine your incongruencies in three categories: meaning, importance, and alignment. Ask yourself:
  - ☐ Am I living in a way that feels meaningful to me?
  - ☐ Am I doing things that are important to me?
  - ☐ Am I aligned with who I imagined myself to be?
- If you notice you're out of harmony, where can you make doable shifts and adjustments?
- Identify and define your anchor (one thing that you can tether yourself to, no matter what is going on in your life). Create a one-line mantra to keep your anchor close to you in difficult moments.

SELF-CHECK-IN QUESTION: Am I living in a way that is consistent with how I see myself?

*Chapter Five*

# STEP 2: TRUST ACCURATELY

When Effie was in first grade, I volunteered in her class every Tuesday to test the kids on their math facts. If you aren't here yet in parenting or are past this stage and don't know what I'm talking about, math facts are basic calculations that the students were asked to memorize so that they could learn to do math quickly. When a kid would pass a particular number, meaning do all the problems correctly and answer each one in three seconds or less, they would graduate to the next math fact.

I really didn't enjoy the insane amount of power this volunteer job gave me. The kids approached my tiny-sized desk in the back-left corner of the room with extreme trepidation. As hard as it is to imagine me being intimidating as I sat twelve inches off the floor with my knees practically beside my earlobes, to them I resembled the gargoyle of math facts. I was perched in my position of power, causing anxiety, and standing between the kids and a feeling of success and mastery of first-grade math.

One thing I did enjoy about Tuesdays was that it gave me an inside glimpse into Effie's life at school. I always felt a little uneasy about the idea of her spending seven-plus hours a day in someone else's care at only six years old, but it's what people do and where kids go, so I told myself to just chill out with my worry. As my husband liked to remind me, "You can't just raise the kids in a bubble." Thanks, babe, that helps.

The thing is, though, Effie had changed in her short time in first grade. The ball-of-fire, bold, courageous, and outspoken girl who first walked through those doors had become anxious, uneasy, and unsure. I chalked most of these changes up to a growing sense of self-awareness that tends to develop around this age. That is, until I witnessed something one Tuesday morning in October.

The teacher had thirty-one students to manage, and it was a hybrid of first and second graders. I felt for her and truly understood the difficulty of teaching all these kids at different levels without much help. One of her tactics to manage the classroom was to use stations. Each group of kids would spend twenty minutes or so at a station, and then she would yell, "Switch!" I was always there for the morning routine as she explained the stations and then watched as the kids quickly scurried to their places. During the first transition of this particular morning, Effie clearly was confused about where to go next. I watched the entire scene take place from my tiny-table lookout. I recognized Effie's confused look immediately, and then I heard the teacher go, "Effie, helloooooooooooooo?!" I perked up, to say the least. The teacher inquired, "Hello, Effie, anyone home?" and she snapped her fingers in the air, waving them in a swishing motion across Effie's face. Effie, along with the entire class, was now frozen and watching the scene take place. "Effie, you look so confused. Get to your next station. Hurry."

My heart sank, my body flooded with emotion, and my head

filled with questions. If this was how she talked to our daughter when I was in the room, how did she talk to her when I wasn't? Was this type of talk responsible for the shift in our daughter's demeanor?

Several months later COVID hit, and distance learning was put in place. Throughout our time at home, I watched our girl return to the Effie I recognized and thought her to be. It was incredible to witness her confidence reappear and to see her step back into her bold disposition. It was mostly because of this visible change that we decided to homeschool moving forward.

However, there was a lingering remnant of her first-grade experience that has taken time to address, which is what Effie calls "being a slowy." Whenever she would be asked to hurry, she would completely shut down, freeze, or drop her head in shame and say, "I'm just a slowy. I don't know what's wrong with me."

What Effie was vocalizing—"I'm a slowy"—is an inside glimpse into her self-concept or her picture of herself in her own mind. She sees herself as someone who is slow, not as someone who sometimes moves slowly as everyone does; instead, she *is* a "slowy."

What Effie did is something we all do starting at a young age and continue to do for the rest of our lives, and that is we form a picture of ourselves in our mind that we use to engage with in the world. This picture shapes the way we see and talk to ourselves.

The ways that I spoke with Effie about being a "slowy" were all about helping her trust herself *more accurately*, to sketch her picture of herself in a way that is in line with reality and helps her see herself in a positive light. This is what I'm going to teach you to do, because one of the most influential aspects of motherhood is how you see yourself, which is how you construct your self-concept or trust picture. Understanding this trust picture and how you can trust yourself accurately is your pathway out of guilt and perfectionism. But first we must define our terms and dig deep into how this picture develops.

## YOUR TRUST PICTURE

Trust is defined as a feeling of *confidence* that comes from your *belief* in someone (or yourself). This feeling then develops into your *attitude* toward another person or even yourself. For example, if your teenager asks to stay out late and you offer up 11 p.m. as a curfew and then they show up at midnight, your trust in them has been affected. Your confidence in them has declined and you have, albeit probably temporarily, a lowered belief in them. This breach in your trust will undoubtedly sour your attitude toward them and likely will change how you handle their next request.

Now, here's the super important part: *your belief in someone comes from a mental picture that you sketch of them.* Think of this as a mental caricature that you create, where some of the qualities of a person are brought to the foreground and even exaggerated and others are shoved to the background and likely minimized. We do this with nearly all people in our lives, including ourselves.

This trust picture is the lens that we use

- to interact with others and ourselves,
- to interpret others' words and behavior as well as our own,
- to develop judgments about others and ourselves, and
- to predict behavior, reactions, and opinions of others and ourselves.

Let me give you an example of this picture at work. Have you ever attempted to mitigate a toddler tantrum through a combination of all your best tricks? You know this feeling of intense anxiety when you are taking your toddler somewhere and you need it to go smoothly, so you anticipate all the potential bumps in the road—and all the potential bumps on the bumps—and plan accordingly?

*This* is your trust picture at play, in the most straightforward and minor way. You have a picture of your tiny tot in your mind, and you know what tends to set your child off. You use this picture to predict all potential issues and then use that knowledge to stuff that diaper bag full of magic and stardust.

When Roy first turned six, we went through a long stretch of him having major outbursts. These were different from Effie's tantrums, which were your run-of-the-mill, possessed, biting, tossing-on-the-floor screaming kind. Nope, Roy's were different entirely. They were more of the verbally abusive type. These verbal lashings occurred multiple times a day and were very hard to handle because they escalated so quickly.

It sounded like this, but imagine it in a volume and tone that requires you to quickly close all the doors and windows for fear the entire neighborhood will hear:

> "Mom, take me to the potty." (He knows how to use the
> potty.)
> "Why am I not in the potty? Why are you not taking me?" (I
> am literally carrying him to the potty.)
> "Why didn't you put me on the potty? Why aren't I dressed?
> Get my clothes. Get them NOOOOOOOOW!"
> "Why didn't you get them?"
> "You're a liar."

Roy's tone and words were so jarring and angry that it was incredibly hard to regulate through these moments. I would take deep breaths, but truly, I wasn't always successful in keeping my cool. The outbursts continued throughout each day around slightly different topics or triggers. They were quickly stealing all my resources, and I hated the way that they sent me scrambling around the house like a pinball trying to meet all his demands.

I needed a plan. I was exhausted and frustrated, and if you could see the trust picture that I sketched of Roy, it looked like a tiny toilet tyrant, red-faced, finger pointing, with his pants around his ankles.

I had to step back and take into consideration all I *know* about Roy and how he operates. This wasn't automatic. My automatic reaction was that I wanted to wave my finger and tell him to respect his mama. But here's an important piece: my belief in Roy, my attitude toward him, is entirely under *my* control. I'm in charge of it. I had to take in what I *know* about him and resketch my picture.

Here's what I know: Roy is a highly sensitive kid and has occasional anxiety, and it comes out as anger. This is actually really common among boys. When I resketched my picture of him based on my *knowing him deeply*, I was able to change my interpretation, assumptions, and behavior around these moments. When I sketched my trust picture *accurately*, I could handle the situation *appropriately*.

I'm happy to report that these outbursts are now few and far between and can almost always be traced to something triggering his worry.

I want this concept of a trust picture to be crystal clear because it is *so* powerful in your relationships with your kids and yourself, so I am going to give you some basic principles about the trust picture and use Roy's story to illustrate them.

Your trust picture

- begins with what you know factually;
- is influenced by what you focus on and what you *think* about what you know;
- shapes your attitude toward yourself and others;
- becomes the lens that impacts your predictions, interpretations, assumptions, and behavior; and
- is something you are in charge of and responsible for.

If you look at the table on the next page you can see how having an accurate trust picture completely changes how I relate to Roy.

Now, imagine if the same grace, understanding, benefit of the doubt, and deep knowing that you extend to your children were

| TRUST PICTURE PRINCIPLES | IF I SEE ROY AS A TINY TOILET TYRANT | IF I SEE ROY AS A KID WITH WORRY |
|---|---|---|
| Begins with what you know factually | Roy screams and barks demands. | Roy screams and barks demands. |
| Is influenced by what you focus on and what you think about what you know | Roy does this because he is disrespectful and demanding. | Roy does this because he feels anxious about something (e.g., being late, having an accident). |
| Shapes your attitude toward yourself and others | I am irritated and angry with him. | I feel compassion and empathy. |
| Becomes the lens that impacts your predictions, interpretations, assumptions, and behavior | I threaten consequences, lecture him about respect and being kind and careful with his words and tone. I continually send the message that he's too much for me to handle. | I teach him self-regulation skills. I help him identify what's triggering his anxiety, help him develop language around it, and talk about it with him, letting him know I'm not afraid of his worry. He isn't too much for me. I set appropriate boundaries regarding his behavior from a regulated place rather than reacting emotionally and giving threats. |
| Is something you are in charge of and responsible for | I am in charge of where I put my focus: I put it on Roy's disrespect and bad behavior. | I am in charge of where I put my focus: I put it on knowing Roy feels anxious. |

reflected back toward you. How would your trust picture of yourself look different if you sketched it with the same love and care as you sketched your children's? When we construct our trust picture of ourselves inaccurately, we experience things like perfectionism and overwhelming guilt. Our self-talk plummets, and we sabotage our ability to care for ourselves in the ways we need. In case you need reminding, I'm going to leave this right here: *we must mother ourselves like we mother our kids*. Keep reading to learn how.

## WHAT STORY ARE YOU
## TELLING YOURSELF?

In Brené Brown's 2019 Netflix special *The Call to Courage*, she summed up the power of a trust picture in the simple phrase "the story I'm telling myself is . . ."[1] This phrase caught like wildfire; it's straightforward and easy to understand and packages complicated concepts into six words. Genius! The thing about the stories we tell ourselves is that they are often inaccurate and lead to our feeling terrible, anxious, guilty, or paralyzed. The solution is to tell an accurate story, to resketch your picture of yourself, just like you do for your kids.

Part of learning how to sketch an accurate picture of yourself is understanding how this picture develops and what sources feed it. I am going to walk you through three sources that feed your expectations of yourself, others, and your circumstances that ultimately develop into the picture you sketch of yourself:

1. Information consumption
2. Societal messaging
3. Early experiences

The three sources spell the acronym "I se." Please grant me the grammatical freedom and pronounce it like "I see."

## 1. Information Consumption

We have never lived with as much accessible information as we do today. We have computers at our fingertips in the form of smartphones. We have parenting, relationship, sleep, and child-feeding experts galore on social media. We have twenty-four-hour news. We have thousands upon thousands of television shows and movies we can watch whenever we want—without commercials. (By the way, you know you're a millennial parent if you've ever said, "When I was little, we had to watch *The Price Is Right* when we stayed home from school sick. We didn't get to watch whatever we wanted." Or some version of the "I walked five miles uphill to school in the snow" lesson that is completely meaningless to our kids.)

This information is a blessing, but almost every blessing comes with a dark side. The dark side is that we are often overwhelmed by all the choices and voices. This overwhelm can fuel the intensive parenting conflict outlined in chapter 1, drawing us further away from our own knowing and closer to the worry that we are getting it wrong or that some expert has the "right" answer. It can also fuel comparison and forms much of what we believe to be ideal experiences in motherhood. This information becomes our measuring stick, it forms our "shoulds," and this can quickly become problematic.

I know you know this experience of getting lost in Google or Instagram for hours on end, digging deep into the internet's trenches, looking for just the right combination of information to get your baby to sleep through the night. "There has to be a way to crack the code," you keep muttering to yourself as you open yet another browser tab on your phone. It's maddening, yet sometimes it's also empowering, so it becomes hard to navigate and know when to stop searching.

## 2. Societal Messaging

Societal messaging consists of all the things we absorb from our culture that impact how we form our expectations of ourselves, others, and our circumstances. This messaging can be subtle and hard to pinpoint, but do know that it exists.

We absorb messages from society about what it means to be a girl and woman, what it means to be a good student, a strong Christian, a success, and so on. These messages are sort of like your body absorbing sunshine and making vitamin D; you're out there soaking it in but not totally aware of what's going on under the surface. It's just automatic. But I'm telling you here and now this happens, so do your best to explore the ways cultural and societal messages have developed into your expectations.

### 3. Early Experiences

If you didn't spend much time thinking about your early experiences with your caregivers in chapter 4, consider again how you were mothered. It doesn't matter if you had a great mom, an absent mom, or an abusive mom—you were influenced by how you were mothered. You take these early experiences and use them to form your list of dos and don'ts as you become a mom. This influences your expectations of yourself as a mother. Don't underestimate the power of a mother's role in your own mothering experience.

This area extends beyond the home. Think of Effie learning in first grade that she is a "slowy." Reflecting back on your early experiences can be eye-opening when it comes to understanding how your expectations developed.

So let's recap because this is a major concept, but it will help you understand your relationships with others and yourself at a much deeper and more practical level.

You have a trust picture that you sketch of yourself (and others). This trust picture begins with what you factually know and is influenced by what you *think* about what you know and what you focus on. This picture shapes your attitude, interpretations, assumptions, and behaviors toward yourself and others. And you are in charge of this trust picture. Your trust picture is formed from three primary sources—information consumption, societal messaging, and early experiences—and these sources help to shape your expectations about yourself and others. I want to help you explore expectations that directly impact how you mother. If you have a hard time determining your expectations, think about the self-talk that starts with "should." This is a dead giveaway.

## STOP SHOULD-ING ON YOURSELF

Something you must know about expectations is that when they differ greatly from what you experience in your reality, guilt, frustration, negative self-talk, and feelings of falling short tend to creep in.

The statement we're going to unpack around expectations is "The type of mom I thought I'd be is . . ." Remember that the ways you answer these questions are influenced by information consumption, societal messaging, and early experiences.

I am going to give you four areas to explore regarding your expectations: attitude, aptitude, appearance, and activity. See the chart on the next page for examples and definitions.

These expectations shape the standards to which you hold yourself and others. When you fall short of meeting these expectations, your trust picture or self-concept becomes negative.

As a side note, I want to mention that a common occurrence for moms is that their birth experience did not go as planned. This sometimes traumatic entry into motherhood can mean that you've fallen short of your expectations right off the bat. This birth trauma can take a long time to process and heal from. These exercises may help you work through some of this disappointment and mistrust,

| AREA OF EXPECTATIONS | DEFINITION | EXAMPLE | EXAMPLE |
|---|---|---|---|
| **Attitude** | Your general disposition in motherhood; your feelings of enjoyment and joy | I will love spending all my time playing with my kids. | I will have endless patience. |
| **Aptitude** | The competence and mastery that you believe you will have in motherhood | I know I will have a finely tuned intuition in motherhood. | I have a plan for parenting and discipline. |
| **Appearance** | What you think you'll look like as a mom; this includes your appearance or even the appearance of your space | I will look put together as a mom. | I will be one of those moms who make it look easy. |
| **Activity** | How you imagine spending your time and the amount of energy you imagine having for activity | I will work part-time while also being a stay-at-home mom. I can juggle both. | I will have the energy to enroll the kids in tons of extracurriculars. |

but you may also require more in-depth examination with a professional counselor or trusted friend.

Allow me to give you a play-by-play of how the combination of all the things I've been laying out for you can unfold.

During that difficult stretch of time when Roy was losing it multiple times a day, I woke up one day determined to have a good morning with our kids. I did all the things: got up a bit early, drank my coffee in peace, prayed, and set my intentions. *This is going to be a good morning*, I said to myself as I gulped that final sip of coffee. I really enjoy our kids and just wanted to take them to breakfast and create a special memory before school. I heard stirring from the bedrooms, and Effie emerged from her room like that character in *The Ring*, her head hung down and her eyes rolling back into her head. She stomped up the stairs and threw herself onto a barstool, immediately going into a whining saga about not wanting to go to school. If you remember, I homeschool, and the kids go to a homeschool "academy" a few days a week. Come on, they *barely* have to *go* to school.

MOM PLAY-BY-PLAY: I had expectations for the morning's activity that I would be doing something fun with the kids and that my attitude would be tip-top chippery-chipper. I was already getting irritated. Effie knew we were going to breakfast, so why the ordeal? My expectations and reality were drifting apart.

Then Roy woke up in his typical fashion by screaming "I'm awake" from his bunk bed. I've been asked why I don't just tell him to come out of his room, but if you have any sense, you already know that a kid who doesn't come out of the bedroom in the morning without your first getting them is the greatest parenting gift ever. Why would I ruin that? Anyway, he immediately went into his "take me potty" hysterics. The kids had been up a mere ten minutes, and I already felt like I had depleted my coping resources.

After going potty, Roy walked over to the couch, where he found Effie slumped over (not getting dressed as I had asked 23,049,390,470 times), and he accidently bumped into her. She lifted her foot and "pushed" him back. He swung. She kicked. They both screamed, and I completely lost it. I yelled, "STOOOOP IT!" and then I did something I hate that I do, which is I narrated my frustration. I talked about how I just wanted to have fun and what's going on this morning and *uuuughhhh*. Yes, an audible groan was how I ended my mom-alogue.

Immediate shame, self-judgment, and feelings of failure rushed in.

MOM PLAY-BY-PLAY: I didn't live up to my own self-imposed expectations. I had a running feed of Instagram experts swirling around in my head (information consumption) that were intensifying my feelings of failure. I had expectations of my aptitude and attitude in these situations. I am an expert, gosh darn it; I should handle these situations flawlessly. A good mom wouldn't lose it on her kids (societal messaging). A good mom doesn't yell (societal messaging, information consumption). A good mom approaches these situations with deep insight and empathy into their children's perspectives. I should have been more patient.

The result of this morning debacle was a deep-felt sense of *I suck at this motherhood thing.* Why? Because my reality and my expectations of myself as a mother were way off. Because my trust picture was highlighting all the gaps in my mothering, the ways I was falling short. The story I was telling myself was that *I should be better at this and I'm not; I am not a good mom; I am ruining my kids' lives; I am a failure of an expert; and also my kids are poorly behaved, and I must make immediate changes in how I parent because clearly I'm doing it wrong.*

This right here is important: how we sketch this picture of ourselves in hard moments will determine how we feel and think about ourselves. When your child is melting down and your trust picture directly connects your child's behavior with your worth and quality as a mother, your self-concept will suffer. This picture we sketch of ourselves in mundane moments is why experiences that should be enjoyable can be robbed of their joy, like when you're walking hand in hand through the grocery store but feeling like you should be doing something more exciting or stimulating. This picture we sketch of ourselves in moments of alone time or self-care is why guilt rushes in when we try to take rest. This picture is powerful. The way you see yourself matters.

So what's next? I know you've been here, too, or if you haven't, someday you probably will. So keep reading.

## A TARGETED APPROACH

The reason I wanted to lead you through all the details of under-standing your trust picture is because each of the areas I described offers an entry point for making changes. You have options.

When it comes to your sources, you are able to make changes. If you're unclear, let me give you some examples in the table below.

| SOURCE | ASK YOURSELF THIS | PUT IT INTO PRACTICE |
|---|---|---|
| **Information Consumption** | *Before I turn to the experts, what do I think?* | Set boundaries around the type of accounts you follow on social media. If you feel worse after you close the app, this is a sign to take a break from information consumption. |
| **Societal Messaging** | *Are there societal messages I'm absorbing that are hurting the way I see myself? Do we moms have a shared negative experience because of these messages?* | Examine what you've absorbed about being a "good" mom from society. Do these standards work for you? If not, then it's time to rewrite these expectations (see section on guilt for how to do this). |
| **Early Experiences (see chapter 4)** | *What do I want to repeat in my family? How can I make this happen?* | Identify things you'd like to change about the family you create. Set one behavioral goal to support this change. |

However, some of the most powerful and quick places for making changes come in the form of changing your focus and altering your expectations.

## ZOOM IN, ZOOM OUT

There are sayings that capture the way our focus impacts our life, like "What you focus on becomes your reality." Or as Brian Tracy said, "The law of concentration states that whatever you focus on grows."[2] These sayings are true; we know this from our lived experiences and from psychological research.

There is a hilarious and famous study conducted by Harvard researchers called the invisible gorilla, which examined attention. The study went something like this: There were three participants wearing all white and three wearing all black—six in total. The white-dressed participants were asked to pass a basketball back and forth. The subject in the experiment was asked to count the number of passes made between the white-dressed players. About thirty seconds into the experiment, a person dressed in a gorilla suit walked through the players and pounded on his chest. Here's the crazy part: 50 percent of the subjects never saw the gorilla because they were so focused on counting the passes.[3] So let me ask you—what gorillas are you missing? What are you so focused on in your own self-concept that you're missing other, arguably, obvious things?

Our focus is one of the most incredible tools when it comes to realigning our trust picture. We can instantly zoom in on something that we are feeling ashamed or guilty about and experience that rush of negative emotion, or we can zoom in on our other qualities and strengths that are fair and more balanced. Remember, we control and are responsible for sketching our trust picture. We can choose where to place our focus.

Sometimes we need to zoom out in order to shift our focus. This may mean reminding ourselves of the big picture—that our relationships with our kids is the totality of lots of small moments, not one moment in time, and that there is room for grace, forgiveness, and repair in our relationships. We can zoom out and offer ourselves gentle reminders that it's normal to feel frustrated or that we all have limitations.

Then we can zoom in on a quality that is actually worth our attention and is a more accurate likeness to who we are and what this moment may be.

I helped Effie zoom out when it came to her self-concept as a "slowy." I helped her see that so many of us experience these moments. I showed her examples of slowness in others and even how I have the same tendency. I told her about how I can putz around the house when I think I have plenty of time to get somewhere just to end up running late because I've used up all my time putzing.

Then I helped Effie zoom in. She was focusing on the negative aspects of moving slowly, but gosh, couldn't we all use a lesson in how to move slowly? There are so many wonderful things about moving slow. Effie literally stops to smell the flowers. It's not always convenient, but I love that about her. We zoomed in on the positive aspects of slowness and differentiated between the times when we may need to move fast and the many more moments when slowness can reign. We resketched her trust picture, zooming out for perspective, then zooming in for a renewed focus. It changed her relationship with slowness and her picture of herself.

In that harried morning I described with the kids, I did the same. I zoomed out and asked myself what was being stirred up in me. Ah, yes, all those things I already described about falling short and not meeting my own expectations. All reflections of me and my shortcomings. Then I shifted my entire focus from *I suck* to *Our kids are having a hard time. They are filled with big emotions and grumpy with each other (that's a normal human experience), and it has nothing to do with me.* I knew I could shift my focus and change the mood of the morning not just for the kids but for myself. Part of this required that we make repairs, and I modeled this for them by saying, "I'm sorry I yelled; that is not how I want to handle frustration." Yes, I moved back toward the expectations I have for myself as a mother, I aligned more with who I believe myself to be (chapter 4), and that felt good. Then we hit reset. I also hit reset for myself, and I focused on all that I did right to repair the relationships. Then I recited (in my head) a mantra that I use to lock in my refocus.

*I'm a good mom. I'm also a mom who makes mistakes, and when I do, I have an opportunity to teach our kids how to fix mistakes.*

Think of this ability to zoom in and zoom out as an in-the-moment strategy for altering your mood and experience. Just like twisting the aperture on a camera lens, you have control over how you frame your perspective of you! It takes some practice, but it can be done in an instant when a hard moment strikes.

> **This ability to zoom in and zoom out is an in-the-moment strategy for altering your mood and experience.**

I just want to call one thing out. There is rampant messaging about how "kids are only young once" or "someday you'll miss this" or "enjoy every moment, mama." Oh, how these messages can haunt us and stir up feelings of inadequacy when we aren't enjoying every moment. Talk about layering guilt on guilt. These messages come from a very zoomed-out perspective; they are big-picture messages.

There are times in your life and in motherhood when big-picture perspectives are helpful and absolutely necessary. But pay attention to when you are mothering from this perspective and feeling bad because of it. If it feels good, by all means, proceed. But if this perspective conjures up more guilt and hardship, zoom in. Twist that lens and pay attention to the moment you're in—the way your toddler waddles with arms outstretched toward you or the sunshine pouring in while you sip your coffee. Zoom in on how you show up every darn day for your kids because you're doing it, and that is something.

## GUILT AND EXPECTATIONS

The other area of intervention is to alter your expectations to be more in line with reality. This brings up the topic of guilt, one of the hottest topics in the motherhood sphere. In the book *Mommy Guilt*, the authors conducted a survey of 1,306 parents, and 95 percent of respondents said they experience feelings of guilt associated with parenting.[4] The thing is, this statistic likely isn't all that surprising to you; it's just familiar.

Let me break down guilt, and I'll show you how it can be relieved not just by shifting your focus but also by altering your expectations. I want you to know that guilt isn't inherently bad. Guilt shows up sometimes to shine a light on something we may need to repair within ourselves or our relationships. But when it weighs you down, keeping you locked in place and unable to care for yourself, or ties you to unproductive, self-criticizing thoughts and talk, it's got to go.

Guilt is a feeling we experience when we've done something wrong. It's found in the gap between who we are and who we think we *should* be. Here's the key: some guilt is deserved and other guilt is undeserved.

Deserved guilt occurs when you've done something wrong. This guilt is productive because it motivates you to repair or make amends. Undeserved guilt is just that; it's guilt that rears its ugly head when you've done nothing wrong. This type of guilt occurs when your expectations have gone to extremes and evolved into impossible standards. Impossible standards are just expectations with the dial turned all the way up. They are more rigid and can sound a little ridiculous, but they play a major role in feelings of guilt. This undeserved guilt is almost always tied to your expectations or impossible standards (expectations gone to extremes) more than it is to reality.

Let me give you some examples.

| IMPOSSIBLE STANDARD | RESULTING GUILT |
| --- | --- |
| If I don't sacrifice all my personal needs for my kids, I'm a bad mom. | I took time to care for myself today, and I couldn't even enjoy it. I felt guilty the entire time. |
| Since I'm a stay-at-home mom and don't "work," I haven't earned the right to ask for help or get a break. | My partner took the kids for a bit, and I felt terrible that I couldn't manage on my own. I needed help, and now I feel terrible that I couldn't handle it alone. I shouldn't be this worn-out; this is all I do. |
| To be valuable, I must have a full plate. | I need help but can't bear the idea of asking anyone or burdening anyone with what I *should* be able to take care of. |

You may read these examples and brush them off as too extreme, but I assure you, if you experience guilt, something along these lines is lurking under the surface.

## REVISING YOUR EXPECTATIONS
## AND IMPOSSIBLE STANDARDS

When examining expectations or impossible standards, it can be helpful to think of yourself as a detective; all you're doing is observing, gathering evidence, and being curious. Why do I suggest this? Because a detective isn't the judge and jury, casting a sentence on you for all your "crimes" in motherhood. A detective just takes it all in. That's the position I'd like you to assume.

The second position I'd like you to assume is one of an experimenter. An experimenter tests out hypotheses but does not shame the hypotheses. An experimenter gathers information and holds it to rigorous testing standards. I want you to do the same.

I am going to give you six basic steps for revising your expectations and impossible standards. I encourage you to grab a pen or pencil and work these out when you have a little time. After you have done this once, you likely will not have to go through the steps so mechanically. Moving forward, after you have identified these buggers, you will be able to quickly call yourself out, examine them in your head, and adjust.[5]

The six steps are as follows:

1. Identify your expectation or impossible standard (detective).
2. Gather evidence that supports it (detective and experimenter).
3. Gather evidence that denies it (detective and experimenter).
4. Revise your standard—maybe it's a compromise, maybe it's dropping it altogether, and maybe your revised standard aligns more with reality after gathering and examining the evidence.
5. Develop a mantra to help you align with the revised standard in the moment.
6. Come up with one or two behavior changes you can implement to support the new standard.

## *Mantras for the Moment*

- What I do is important and sometimes difficult; it makes sense if I feel tired and need help.
- I'm not a bad mom; my child is having a hard time.
- The quality of our relationship isn't defined by one moment of me being off.
- I'm a good mom. It's normal for me to feel [overwhelmed, frustrated, exhausted].
- I am a good mom *and* have a need for time alone.

Why, oh why do I ask you to make a behavioral change? The short story is that your behavior can facilitate changes in your thoughts *and* feelings, just like changing your thoughts and feelings can help to move your behavior. Behavioral change will solidify your change of thoughts and feelings. Oftentimes we need to be encouraged to make a behavioral change before we *feel* ready. So just do it.

Take a look at the example I've given you on the next page.

Now you try. Do this for as many impossible standards as you can come up with. You can scan the QR code to access a printable version of this table. Tip: if you need help remembering reasons why caring for yourself is important, return to chapter 2 and read my case for your care.

**IMPOSSIBLE STANDARD:** *Since I am a stay-at-home mom and don't "work," I haven't earned the right to ask for help or get a break.*

| EVIDENCE FOR | EVIDENCE AGAINST | REVISED STANDARD |
|---|---|---|
| No one *offers* me a break. | Every working person gets a break. | Since I am a stay-at-home mom, it is important that I get breaks and help when I need it. I may have to ask for what I need, but that doesn't mean my contribution is less valuable. |
| I keep being told how lucky I am to stay home with my kids. | Taking care of kids is exhausting and requires a lot of emotional regulation. It isn't realistic to do this without breaks. | |
| I don't feel valued for what I do. | Other moms take breaks, and I don't think less of them. | |

**IN-THE-MOMENT MANTRA:** *I am doing an incredibly important job, and it requires that I take care of myself.*

**ZOOM IN OR ZOOM OUT:** I will zoom out and remind myself of all the other moms who take breaks, which I support. I will zoom in on the ways that I love and nurture our children and how I give them all they need and remind myself that taking breaks doesn't take away from all that I do.

**BEHAVIORAL CHANGE:** I will ask my partner to take the kids once a week for a couple of hours so I can do what I choose with that time.

## TRUST ACCURATELY

Trust is your *feeling* of confidence that stems from your *belief* in yourself or others. This belief comes from a picture that you sketch of yourself or someone else. When you sketch this picture, you exaggerate some qualities and minimize others. This can be detrimental to your well-being, depending on where you zoom in.

The sources that influence how you sketch this picture and form your expectations and impossible standards come from the information you consume, how you've been shaped by societal messages, and what you've learned from your early life experiences.

The expectations and impossible standards that you hold for yourself today may not serve you. They may not be aligned with reality and may be tethering you to a past way of living and mothering that sabotages your ability to find joy and peace in motherhood.

## *Go Mom Yourself*

### Step 2: Trust Accurately

- Mother yourself like you mother your kids by giving yourself the same attention, care, and benefit of the doubt as you sketch your trust picture.
- Zoom out and zoom in when necessary, which allows you to focus on what you're doing well and stop dwelling on things that suggest you're falling short.
- Examine your expectations and impossible standards so that you can reality-check them, revise them, and see yourself in a positive light.
- Develop a mantra for a quick, in-the-moment reset.

SELF-CHECK-IN QUESTION: Am I seeing myself in a positive light?

*Chapter Six*

# STEP 3: RELY BOLDLY

**U**se your words. I'm almost certain you've said this to one of your kids, and if you haven't, you've thought it. These three words, just three syllables, express a desire to know your kid's needs.

I know I've said these before. Four-year-old Effie was flat on her belly wailing away in some very public place. I was bending down, feeling exasperated with no accessible tools to handle the sheer intensity of the tantrum and embarrassed by the public display, so I leaned in and said, "Can you *just* use your words?" My plea was drawn out and desperate. Clearly, Effie was emotional. Clearly, there was something going on. Clearly, something didn't feel good for her. But what was it? What did she need? I had to know so I could make her feel better. So come on, child, "Use your words."

When the moment was over and my mind and the audience

had cleared, I knew that it was a big ask. Little kids can't articulate what they need when they're dysregulated—and adults aren't much better. In fact, little kids don't always know what they need, but it's one of our roles as a parent to help them define their needs and learn how to assert them.

When Effie was eight, she started wondering out loud to me why her aunt didn't initiate alone time with her. My sister is four years younger than I am and had recently relocated with her husband and two-year-old son to California from New York. She is thoughtful yet sometimes can miss the big picture because of the intensity of the in-the-moment stuff.

I believe my sister's lack of initiation was more about the pace of her life with a toddler, the overwhelm of carrying it all, and the need to protect her energy and get some rest. It had nothing to do with her lack of desire to be with Effie or spend time with her. Yet I'll admit, it was difficult to hear my child notice this and express hurt because of it. Effie said to me once, "One day I'll be grown, and she'll realize she missed her chance to be close to me." Someone hand me the tissues.

These types of big conversations with your little kids are hard to prepare for. The smallness of their stature contrasted with the gravity of their words is heavy. The weight of the responsibility for managing these formative moments instantly reminds me of the immense privilege it is to raise children and the power we have as parents to help guide them as they handle themselves and their relationships.

If you remember, Effie is a "slowy." We had to process and discuss this specific predicament for a very long time. The topic would arise, seemingly out of nowhere, and she would want to discuss it. We explored what it feels like for her. I dug into my sister and how she thinks and operates, helping Effie understand her perspective and intention. I wanted her to see my sister's heart behind the hurt that it was causing Effie. My sister didn't mean to hurt her feelings, but she had. This is often the case with unexpressed needs: it hurts, but the other person doesn't even know it's happening.

After a thorough analysis, we got to a place where I asked Effie if she wanted to do something about it. "I'm worried that if I tell her she has hurt me, I will hurt her feelings. I'm worried she will be upset with me for hurting her."

For a moment can you just reflect on those unfiltered and raw words from an eight-year-old? I love how children approach things with such vulnerability and fearlessness. Her worry was so relatable. *If I ask for something I need, I'm worried I'll inconvenience you, stir up defensiveness in you, or upset you. I'm worried my need will be too much for you and you will not be able to meet it, so maybe I should just make my need smaller.* I know this worry. I'm sure you know it too.

We had a rich discussion around expressing our needs. We talked about how when we keep our needs hidden or small, people don't know how to love us in the ways that we need. That when we keep our needs secret, it's harder to get them met. And that our job in a relationship is to express our needs, and then it's up to the other person to decide what to do with it. That's not in our control; it's in theirs. If her aunt got upset with her for expressing her need, then that wasn't Effie's fault—she did her job. It would be her aunt's job to receive the need and ultimately choose how to respond. We talked about ways of telling her, we prepared scripts, and we considered how she would handle disappointment.

A month later we were at a family dinner. Effie came up to me and said, "That's it; I have to talk to her. I can't wait." And so she did. She pulled my sister aside and said, "I really would love to spend some special time alone with you. Do you think we could do that?" And my sister responded, "I've been thinking about that too. I have some ideas."

That was a magic moment for Effie. And truly, it was for me

too. I watched our daughter's need rise to the surface of her awareness, I listened to her evaluate it, I watched her confront her fear of sharing it, I observed her courage in expressing it, and I saw her stamp down that all-to-common tendency for us to make our needs small and palatable to others. She found her strong voice, and I couldn't be happier. She boldly expressed her needs.

This is what you, as a mom, must learn to do. You are not meant to shoulder so much of the responsibility without room to breathe, the chance to reset, and the opportunity to pursue something that brings you joy. You must learn to rely boldly on others, to take up space, and to articulate your needs; however, women in general, and moms more specifically, struggle with this.

> **You must learn to rely boldly on others, to take up space, and to articulate your needs.**

In "Balance Is Baloney" I talked about a core conflict moms face: sacrificing our identity or our needs versus the needs of everyone else. This conflict highlights the tendency for moms to sacrifice our needs for the preservation of our relationships. Whether it's learned or innate, we start this from a young age, just like Effie vocalized "I'm worried my need will upset my relationship with my aunt."

Moms struggle with needs because we want to maintain peace and harmony in the home and in our lives. It feels easier to self-sacrifice than to assert our voices. Yet there is a dramatic cost to this. We build frustration and resentment toward others and develop burnout trying to exist without needs.

In this chapter I'm going to help you explore two primary areas that shape how comfortable you are with asserting your needs and relying on others. These two areas are your attachment style and how your expression of needs has been received in past relationships. Then I will help you to explore what your needs are and how you can develop more comfort around asserting those needs in your relationships.

## ATTACHMENT STYLES 101

"Morgan, I need to talk to you soon about your reel today," my mom said to me in a hurried tone. I laugh as I even write this. The idea that Instagram and short, silly videos have such an impact on my life just blows my mind. My kids come to me with reel ideas, they integrate funny audio into their jokes, and they ask to watch them and rate them, *Gladiator*-style, thumbs-up or thumbs-down. It's ridiculous, but as we all say when we don't know what to say, *It is what it is.*

The reel that my mom was referring to was about attachment styles. It was simple: I was rocking a baby while words popped up about attachment theory and the different styles that came out of this research. I picked up the phone and called my mom. She said, "Oh my gosh, I'm avoidant. Everything is clicking for me now. Can we talk about it when the kids go to bed?"

Who knew that one silly thirty-second reel would lead to deep insight for my mom, her understanding of her attachment style, and how it impacts the way she shows up in her relationships? Wild.

Attachment theory was pioneered by John Bowlby in the 1950s and is one of the most influential theories of our time. Bowlby was a British psychologist who studied child development and focused on the child–primary caregiver (usually the mother) relationship. The premise of attachment theory is this: our early experiences with our caregivers and how they respond to our needs have a major impact on how we form attachments to others throughout the course of our lives. Based on his observations and research, Bowlby developed four attachment styles: secure, anxious, avoidant, and disorganized.[1]

His work was furthered by his student Mary Ainsworth, who structured a famous experiment called the strange situation. Here's the gist of this experiment: Children ages nine months to thirty months old were brought into an observational room with toys, and then they were exposed to a situation with different degrees of stressfulness. Specifically, they entered the room with a parent, a stranger entered and spoke to the parent, the parent left, and the child was alone with the stranger. Then the parent returned.

The experimenters observed several key areas: how the children explored on their own, how the children reacted when their parent left, how anxious they seemed with a stranger in the room, and how the children reacted when their caregiver returned. Based on these observations, the researchers saw patterns in how the children reacted when their caregiver was gone and then returned. These patterns helped Ainsworth elaborate on Bowlby's original attachment styles (see table on the next page).[2]

Please note that there are all sorts of nuanced variations of attachment styles. There are entire books written on this theory and even self-help books on how it impacts relationships.[3] I'm going to provide a simple breakdown that gives you enough to get the concepts and explore for yourself without getting too technical.

I'm sure you can imagine the possible reactions of these poor children subjected to the research of curious psychologists. Crying, ignoring, clinging, confusion, and confidence. But through this research an important discovery was made about how we create internal pictures of what our external reality looks like. As young children we internalized templates from our caregivers based on how those caregivers responded to our needs. We use this internalized template to anticipate how others will respond to us, what we can expect from them, and whether our needs will or won't be met. These templates are our shortcuts, the lenses through which we see others, and they were developed at a very young age.

| ATTACHMENT STYLE | PARENTING LIKELY SEEMED | RELIANCE ON SELF | RELIANCE ON OTHER | KEY FEATURE | HOW THIS SHOWS UP IN REGARD TO NEEDS |
|---|---|---|---|---|---|
| Secure | Responsive, sensitive, loving | High | High | Gives and receives love easily | High confidence that others will meet their needs; comfortable expressing their needs |
| Anxious | Inconsistent and unpredictable | Low | High | Needs reassurance; wonders, *Will you be there for me?* | Low confidence that others will meet their needs; desires closeness |
| Avoidant | Insensitive and rejecting | High | Low | Seems dismissive; wonders, *Will you take my independence?* | Low confidence that others will meet their needs; desires independence |
| Disorganized | Erratic, frightened, or frightening | Low | Low | Feaful and confusing; inconsistent | Has no strategies to get their needs met |

The technical term for these templates is *mental representations.* Later research has found that our attachment style is fairly stable throughout the course of our lifetime and impacts the way that we show up in our adult relationships.[4]

Let me pause for a moment because I'm intuiting your panic that you may have messed up your child's attachment style. Is your kid anxious? *Oh no, I created an avoidant when I went to dinner with my friends that one night.* I get it, sometimes information can feel overwhelming and defeating.

Try to pivot your perspective to this: *information is meant to be empowering, not entrapping.* Information like this can offer us insight into ourselves, our relationships, and our children. It can embolden us to observe our proclivities in our relationships from a different perspective, make changes, and shift toward a more secure way of relating. We can also nurture this in our children.

Okay, let's take the concept home by completing the story of my mom's attachment revelation. I've shared already that my mom was adopted at two months old. She was welcomed into the home of a cold and distant woman who was highly gregarious with others but not with her own child. My mom describes her childhood as being very lonely. When my mom was five years old, her parents adopted a two-year-old boy who was later diagnosed with schizophrenia. He struggled with mental health issues throughout his entire growing up and received the concern, love, and attention that my mom craved. Simply put, my mom was rejected by her birth mother then neglected by her adoptive mother.

When she called me that day and said, "I'm avoidant!" she was right. It was a massive light bulb moment for her. She recognized why she retreats and disconnects when she feels threatened or worries that she will be abandoned. If you took her internal template and plopped it on the table and listened to it, these are just some of the things it would say.

- *I have to be self-reliant because others do not show up for me.*
- *I feel jealous when my loved ones have close relationships with others because it means that they are abandoning me.*
- *When I feel unsafe, I need to reject others before they reject me.*
- *When I feel threatened that a loved one won't show up for me, I want to escape the relationship.*
- *My needs don't matter.*

Our attachment style is something we bring with us into all our relationships. When it is activated, we may have the desire to run, seek reassurance, hide, lash out, and so on. Your attachment style tells you what you can expect from others when you need something from them, and if your attachment style is such that you don't trust that people will be there for you, the ways that you go about trying to get your needs met may not be productive. You may engage in relationship-sabotaging or even self-sabotaging behaviors.

Guess what happens when my mom retreats because of fear of abandonment? She disconnects and is alone. She creates the circumstances that she fears. How powerful for her to notice this tendency and be able to say, "When I need someone, instead of leaning into the fear that they won't show up, I will assert what I need." This is how you approach your attachment style differently. You notice it, learn from it, and change your behavioral responses.

Meeting needs is an exchange between people. This is part of what makes expressing needs so scary; having your needs met requires that others show up for you, that they hear you and value you and are willing to respond in a way that lets you know you are important to them. When we express our needs and are met with defensiveness, rejection, or accusations of neediness, our internal templates are substantiated. *See, no one is there for me. See, no one cares enough about me to care for me.*

Knowing your relationship tendencies based on your attachment style can help you to assess how you rely on others. Please know that the goal is a healthy reliance on others, or interdependence. If you imagine a continuum, on one end is detachment and on the other is codependency. Codependency is just extreme dependence or reliance; it is defining yourself through your relationship. Extreme detachment is the feeling that *I don't need anyone.* Try to identify where you are on this continuum and imagine what a healthy interdependence looks like. When you have a healthy interdependence, it fosters more secure independence. It feels like *I'm safe to ask for what I need and depend on others, and I can do the same for them.*

## Dependency Continuum

DETACHMENT                                    CODEPENDENCY

To start exploring how your attachment style impacts the ways you express reliance and your needs in relationships, check out the following questions:

- When I imagine asking for a need to be met, what do I think will happen?
- When I sense someone won't be there for me, how do I respond?
- Do I tend to minimize my needs because I anticipate that they will cause a rupture in my relationship?

- How do my attachment tendencies show up in the ways I assert my needs? Are my attachment tendencies helping or hurting my relationships?
- What is one behavioral change I can make in my relationships when it comes to expressing my needs?

## THE THREE PRIMARY RESPONSES TO NEEDS

In an especially challenging time with Roy, I reached out to my closest friend for some advice. I felt completely lost. His screaming episodes were occurring multiple times a day, Chad was traveling so I didn't have backup, and I was beaten down and depleted. During one of Roy's particularly colorful toilet rants, I pulled out my phone and recorded his screaming without his knowing. I wanted my friend to hear it and give me some feedback.

He howled, "Take my sock off NOOOOOOW, do it NOW, why aren't you doing it? I need a new sock. Get it NOOOOW." Sheesh. I felt like I should approach him, straighten my bow tie, and bow like a stinkin' butler. Yes, Roy, sir. Sorry, sir.

I hated that feeling.

Later, when my friend had a chance to listen and send me her impression, she said, "He's telling you exactly what he needs. He's just saying it very loudly, and that sounds like anxiety, like sensory overload."

I already knew that anxiety was playing a big piece in his outbursts, but the statement that "he's telling you exactly what he needs" really struck me. Because he was—he couldn't be clearer. He wanted new socks, and he wanted them yesterday.

I breathed deeply as I walked to get Roy's socks and changed them as he sat on the toilet. He regulated and said, "Thank you."

There are lots of opportunities for picking this story apart: Like how we've had to talk with Roy about why it's hard to see his worry when he delivers the message with anger. Or that we have worked to cultivate more tools for him to handle these moments of overwhelm.

But for a minute, imagine that I responded like this: "Roy, stop it! Stop it right now. You're disrespecting me, and you will *not* talk to me this way. Deal with the dang sock. You're fine."

If you have responded to your kids before in a similar way to what I just described, I want to nudge you to lean into self-compassion. I also want you to know that my skin is not as thick as steel. My kids feel things in big ways, and so do I. And this means that I do not always get it right either. These moments are hard, and we don't always have a textbook response. It's okay. Good enough, remember?

But let's say I responded in these ways almost every time. When a big need would rise up in Roy, what if I continued to send the message to "just deal with it"? Or "Geez, you're too much. Chill out"? Over time Roy would learn that in order to receive a positive appraisal from me, he'd have to shut down his needs. He would learn that he was too much and that he needed to be quieter, smaller, and almost needless. Or he may learn that to get my attention or responsiveness, he would have to increase his use of anger because anger is more effective than crying or talking. Do you know any adults like this?

We've all received messages about our needs growing up and in our adult relationships. Both are formative. Both of these sources of feedback shape how we feel about our needs, what we should do with them, and how we think of ourselves as someone who has these needs.

We receive three primary responses to our needs, and these responses have a dramatic impact on how we ultimately learn to express our needs. So consider, when you've expressed your needs in relationships, with which of these responses were those needs met?

1. MINIMIZED OR CRITICIZED: Your needs were ignored, made to feel silly, met with an irritated response, or patronized.

2. CATEGORIZED: You were accused of being a particular way because of a need you expressed.
3. LEGITIMIZED: You expressed a need, and it was taken seriously and validated (even if it wasn't met).

Let me give you some examples of what each of these sounds like.

## MINIMIZED OR CRITICIZED

- "Ugh, again [eye roll]?"
- "Suck it up."
- "You've got nothing to worry about. Just quit worrying."
- "You love school; get in there."
- "I have no idea what the big deal is about this. What's your problem?"
- "Do you know how good you have it? You need to stop complaining."
- "Just do one thing at a time. Don't stress."
- "Control the controllables."

## CATEGORIZED

- "You're so ungrateful; it's never enough for you."
- "Gosh, you're so defensive. Just admit you're wrong."
- "Wow, you're so sensitive."
- "You are so needy.
- "You're clingy. Get off of me."

## LEGITIMIZED

- "I hear that you're hurting. Let me give you a hug."
- "It sounds like you need more freedom. Let's brainstorm some ways to make that happen."

- "You're missing me and want more one-on-one time. Let's schedule time together."
- "I wonder if you're feeling worried. Let's talk about this."
- "You wish you could stay longer; leaving fun places is hard for me too."
- "You need more reassurance. I understand that my taking this trip is stirring up insecurity; that makes sense."

Again, this book isn't about adding more pressure or opportunities for you to criticize your parenting. Nope. We all say these things from time to time. Mothering at a high intensity all the time isn't sustainable or obtainable. You've likely said one or more of the statements above. I have too.

My point is this: if this way of responding is the rule and not the exception, you may be conveying some messages about needs that you don't intend. And if you have heard these in your own growing-up experiences and relationships, it's likely that you will struggle with defining, owning, and asserting your own needs.

Remember, information should be empowering, not entrapping. When you have defined your experiences, you are equipped to decide where you'd like to make changes and adjustments. I also hope that this information helps to explain why you may struggle to assert yourself. It's not that there's something wrong with you; instead, you may have learned that it gets you nowhere or that it hurts when you do. Use these three responses to explore the messages about expressing your needs that you received early on and then later in your adult relationships.

Think of it like this: your attachment style is like your road map. If you're secure, you'll view your map and terrain a little differently than if you had anxious or avoidant tendencies. All the maps are trying to get you to the same place (closeness, security, and safety), but the route looks different. Your early experiences and the ways your needs were handled (minimized, criticized, categorized, or legitimized) will be the detours and roadblocks along your journey. These will be the extra issues you will have to confront and work around as you try to reach your final destination as someone who expresses needs assertively and relies boldly on others.

Use this first section of the chapter to dig into the reasons why you may be reluctant to assert yourself and your needs. Explore what may be getting in the way of your reliance on others and what you anticipate in terms of whether others will meet your needs or let you down.

## HAVING NEEDS DOESN'T MAKE YOU NEEDY

When I talk with women about their struggles with their needs, their answers always fall into one of three categories. In this section, I want to address all three so that no matter your hang-up when it comes to needs, I've got you covered.

I am going to offer you three things:

1. PERMISSION to have needs
2. DEFINITION around what your needs are
3. EXPRESSION, meaning the tools to articulate and communicate your needs clearly

### Permission

Just because you have needs doesn't mean you are needy. You are not an island. You are wired to connect in relationship to others, and part of that is the need to depend on both yourself and others to have your needs met. I know you received messages throughout your life that suggested you should not burden others, that you should be small, that a good mother martyrs herself for her children. But these messages have been taken to the extreme. They are misleading and self-sabotaging.

We all know that when we birth babies, we birth bundles of

needs. Even as they become toddlers and kids, their need for us (or snacks) doesn't go away. It changes. But what often happens is that the intensity of their needs is so big that ours get crowded out; we move our needs to the background and bring our children's, and everyone else's, to the foreground.

You once were that baby, born into this world with all those needs. You needed connection, love, reassurance, closeness, affection, attention, appreciation, and overall nurture. Your needs were still there when you were a toddler and then a kid and then a teen. What on earth makes you think that as you entered into motherhood those needs suddenly disappeared? Would you want your kids to do the same with their needs?

This is your permission to have needs. I am giving you the go-ahead to tune in to you, challenge your hang-ups about your needs, and finally discover what will fill you up, where you need extra hands, what you need to hear, and how much of all those things you need. If this permission doesn't cut it, let me explain the gravity of needs in the framework of a simple psychological theory called social exchange theory.

Social exchange theory takes an economical approach to understanding relationship exchanges or mutual need fulfillment. This theory incorporates the ideas of rewards and costs. The more rewards one feels in a relationship, the more satisfaction that's derived from the relationship. The more cost one experiences, the more dissatisfaction. The balance between the cost and rewards in relationships dramatically impacts how people experience a relationship and how happy they are in it.[5]

We all derive rewards from motherhood, like the fun of our children and the immense love we feel—I know you know what I mean. But we also incur exorbitant costs, which makes sense because the relationship is not one of equal exchange. We can't expect our children to pour into us like we pour into them. However, it also makes sense that we may feel some discontent and dissatisfaction in the relationship if we're pouring so much into our children without recouping rewards anywhere else. The more self-deprived we are, the more dissatisfied we'll feel in motherhood.

Unlike some other relationships that are on equal terms, motherhood requires that you supplement in other ways. This means that you feel some level of entitlement to have needs, take ownership of what you need, and assert your needs as they arise.

Permission has been granted to have needs. Now, it's important for you to understand that needs change in two ways: they grow in intensity, and they change type completely. This is significant because it requires that you occasionally reassess your needs. After you become a mother, your needs change. During different stages of motherhood, undoubtedly they change again. This is normal.

## 1. THEY GROW IN INTENSITY.

"So I need to compliment you more?" Chad asked me during one ill-timed conversation. In my early years in motherhood, I would bottle up my needs and then blow up at really inopportune times— like before sex or bed or when Chad had just returned from a work trip. "Noooo," I groaned. That wasn't it. I could tell he wanted to roll over and go to sleep and pray this was just a nightmare.

At the time I didn't understand how to articulate what I needed. I had the need to be told I was valuable to him in a way that let me know that he saw all that I did and contributed to our relationship and family. I had this need from the start of our relationship, but after becoming a mother, it dramatically intensified. I needed to hear expressions from Chad that he was able to see the value I added to our family and that all that I did was visible to him. I know how to ask for it now, but at the time, I struggled to define it.

"I do compliment you," he defended himself. "Don't I tell you how good of a mom you are?"

"Yes, I guess you do. Okay, never mind." I rolled over and cried out of frustration and sheer exhaustion.

He wasn't doing anything wrong really; he just wasn't understanding what I needed and felt like he was already doing it. I wasn't clearly articulating what I needed and didn't express the normalcy of needs growing in intensity.

Here's what I want you to know: sometimes you just need *more* of what you are *already* getting.

This realization and phrasing can make all the difference for you and for when you express your needs to others. Yes, you're getting this need met, but maybe you need it met a little more. And that's not just okay; it's normal.

## 2. THEY CHANGE TYPE COMPLETELY.

The second way that needs change is in type. Sometimes what we need now is different from what we needed before. After kids, I need silence. This was new for me. It was a nonissue before. Now it was major.

Because needs change in type, you must check in with yourself on occasion and reevaluate what you need. It also requires that you express to others what you need. This helps them love you and care for you in ways that are actually effective and helpful.

## Definition

I'm reminded of that scene in *The Notebook* where Noah, Ryan Gosling's character, says to Allie (Rachel McAdams), "What do you want?" and she just shakes her head. "What do you want?" he asks again, and finally she replies, "It's not that simple."

This is how it can feel sometimes when you're asked what you need. You may not really know. Just like I didn't know when I was trying to express to Chad that I needed to feel valued and visible.

This is never clearer than when you feel overwhelming confusion about what to do when you finally have a minute to yourself. Do you do laundry, clean, read a book you've been putting off, watch a show, nap, shower, send an email, call a friend, or sit and stare at the wall? By the time you settle into something, your time is usually up.

If you do settle into something, it is often sabotaged by restlessness. You wonder if this is the best way to use your time. You leave your time feeling like it was just a drop in the bucket of what you actually needed. Your level of depletion makes it so hard to define what will really fill you up.

We often feel this deficit but don't have the framework to define it. I am going to give you five categories of needs that can help you outline what you need. The five areas spell out the word LEAPP. I intentionally created this as an acronym so that when you are in the moment and need to evaluate your needs, you can recall these five categories. This will help you target what is missing at the time so you can boldly and clearly express it to your partner, community of support, or yourself.

I will give you examples to help get you started. Then I want you to grab a notepad (when you have the time and space) and write down the needs you have now in each of these categories.

| NEEDS CATEGORIES | EXAMPLES |
|---|---|
| **Logistical** | Tasks of life to be handled, time away, childcare, more done around the house |
| **Emotional** | Togetherness, support, validation, deep conversation, community |
| **Affirmational** | To be seen, valued, and appreciated in words and deeds |
| **Purposeful + Spiritual** | To have a hobby, engage in something you love, creativity, worship, solitude to pray |
| **Physical** | Exercise, massage, quiet, space, sex |

## Expression

I've said a phrase about expressing needs over a hundred times on Instagram, on podcasts, and in workshops, and now I'm saying it to you. If you're expressing a need to yourself or others, *be clear or else you're just confusing.*

I whirled around Chad, huffing and puffing, picking up LEGOs and throw pillows, folding blankets, and narrating the endless list of stuff I still needed to do that no one else seemed to notice. He kindly but firmly said, "Stop. Tell me what you need me to do." I just threw my arms up as if to say, "Look around, my friend, at all of this."

He responded, "I don't know what that means." I said, "I need help with the house." He sighed and said, "When you say that, I do look around, and I think, *Hey, it looks pretty good in here*, so if you have things you want taken care of, I don't see them. Tell me *specifically*, and it's as good as done."

Now, I can imagine your eyes rolling. I know the pushback of having to spell things out to your partner—that's for another book. But know that Chad's feedback came from a good place and a good heart. And it was wise. I was being angry and busy, but I certainly wasn't being expressive or specific. I stopped and explained the list, and he did it *all*. Done.

So when I say "be clear," I mean get really specific with what you need. This may require some self-examination and self-reflection because what you need will change day to day and even moment to moment. And know that in the beginning if you're someone who has a hard time identifying your needs, this may feel really challenging. Practice, practice, practice, and you will get good at it.

Use the chart on the next page and the five categories of needs again, but this time practice coming up with specific things you'd want. Imagine you have time and personnel support to make it happen. What would you *specifically* need in this moment?

| NEEDS CATEGORIES | THE NEED I HAVE | THE SPECIFIC WAY I WANT THIS NEED MET |
|---|---|---|
| Logistical | | |
| Emotional | | |
| Affirmational | | |
| Purposeful + Spiritual | | |
| Physical | | |

## Conquer Your Hang-Ups and Rely Boldly

Conquering your hang-ups and relying boldly may be new to you. This lesson was one I learned gradually over time after I became a mother, and I knew I had no choice but to learn it. I could either become bold with expressing my needs or become bitter in my heart.

Two signs clued me in that I needed to make a change. One, I was walking around the house rage cleaning and muttering about how I didn't get a break. And two, I was starting to resent my husband for taking breaks or having rest. I remember standing in the space between our kitchen and our living room and looking over at a sink full of dishes and then back at Chad, who was taking a power nap on the couch. I remember thinking, *Why am I so mad?*

*Chad will wake up and do the dishes, but I resent that he's power napping.* I was telling myself a story that said, *He thinks I'll just take care of the dishes, and how nice for him that he doesn't carry or feel the weight of that responsibility. How nice he can choose to just leave them and take a nap.*

Not only was my story inaccurate, but it didn't serve me. This was my realization: I could choose too. I could choose to step away and come back to the dishes when I had the energy or even let Chad do them later. I could choose to care for me instead of the home or anyone else in that moment. I didn't have to keep grinding through task after task.

When I took that realization and started to hold it up to other areas of my life, I realized that if I didn't choose my care, I was putting it in the hands of others. Somehow I had outsourced my care to my husband or even my parents. I wanted others to initiate caring for me: "Hey, you go take a walk or a nap or a seven-day Caribbean cruise; we've got the kids and all of life's responsibilities." But asserting what I needed, that was actually my job.

From that moment on, I made a decision to consciously choose how I spend my time and to assert what I need boldly. I finally got out of the booster seat and firmly planted my butt in the driver's seat of my needs. It's been life-changing.

If I see the dishes, I decide if I want to do them now or later. Sometimes they sit longer, but they always get done eventually. I check in with me before tackling these tasks, and I can truly say that now I do them with so much more lightness. The disclaimer here is that life happens, and sometimes it's not feasible to let things slide or power nap on the couch; but when you feel that swelling up of inner rage and frustration that you're not getting the care you need, you know that it's time to reevaluate how you make these choices moment to moment.

The next piece was asserting my needs. When I stepped into an ownership role of my needs, I was better able to begin saying, "Today

| HANG-UP AROUND NEEDS: | | |
|---|---|---|
| **EVIDENCE FOR** | **EVIDENCE AGAINST** | **REVISION** |
| | | |
| | | |
| | | |
| IN-THE-MOMENT MANTRA: | | |
| ZOOM IN AND ZOOM OUT: | | |
| BEHAVIORAL CHANGE: | | |

I need some quiet; how can we make that happen?" Or "This weekend I really need time to connect with friends. Let's prioritize that." The wild part is my husband has given me zero pushback. What took me so long? My hang-ups around needs were self-sabotaging, I outsourced the initiation of my care to others, and I didn't realize the freedom I had to choose how I spend my time.

I want to encourage you to examine these themes and how they show up in your life, getting in the way of your ability to assert your needs. Scan the QR code on the next page to challenge your hang-ups. The mantra piece is especially important. I realize that this can seem a little cliché; however, in the moment when you are struggling to assert your needs and these hang-ups resurface, this mantra will quickly come to mind and give you the guts you need to stay true to the course and rely boldly.

## SPEAK UP

One of my favorite ways to help people in their relationships is to give them scripts. Sometimes we just need to know how to word something. Because relying boldly often requires involving someone else's help, we have to know how to speak up and articulate what we need.

Here are a few rules of thumb for asserting your needs:

- Try to balance assertiveness with grace and compliments. Assertiveness doesn't have to mean gruff or angry.
- Be clear and specific (but you should know this by now).
- Try not to blame or be critical.
- Use the positive approach of asking for more of something rather than the negative "you never do this" approach.

Here are some scripts to get you started:

## TO A PARTNER:

- I haven't been good at expressing what I need, and I fear I'm burning out because if it. You may notice some changes in me speaking up more. I'm happy to talk about it, but just know I'm going to try to be clearer and more direct about what it is that I need.

- I love how you take care of me by _____; would you be able to do that more often?
- I appreciate all you do to show me that you love me, but I feel the most loved when you _____.
- I'm noticing that I am getting irritated more easily. I know this means I need _____. How can we make that happen this week?
- Our schedule and all I'm carrying feels unsustainable. Let's set up a time to talk and find a better distribution.

## TO YOURSELF:

- In this moment, what I need is _____.
- How can I shift my energy today to better meet one of my needs?
- What moments in my day allow for time or space to get a need met?
- How can I choose differently today so I meet a need that I have?
- What can I let go of that will free up space and energy to meet one of my needs?

My wish for you from this chapter is that you have increased your insight into what gets in the way of you asserting your needs. I hope that you combat those hang-ups head-on and replace them with statements that are more accurate and forgiving. I hope that you feel that you have gained permission to take charge of initiating your own care, feel equipped to define what your needs are, and feel emboldened to express them.

# *Go Mom Yourself*

### Step 3: Rely Boldly

- Increase your insight into your hang-ups around needs and revise them to be more realistic.
- Define what your needs are, and come up with clear and specific ways to meet these needs.
- Develop a healthy sense of entitlement around expressing and asserting your needs.
- Make deliberate choices through your day with regard to your needs versus the needs of others.
- Take ownership of initiating your needs, and practice asserting them to yourself and others so they can love you and you can love yourself in the ways that matter most.

SELF-CHECK-IN QUESTION: What do I need the most?

# Chapter Seven

## STEP 4: COMMIT WISELY

**B**ut I can't bring all my toys!" exclaimed Effie. I inhaled and tried to calm my anxiety. Chad and the kids were supposed to leave forty minutes earlier to head to the mountains for the weekend so I could write. These weekends were when I would get my best thinking and writing done, and I saw my time and my energy quickly slipping away. "You are allowed to take any toys you want with you, Effie. Are you sure that's all that's upsetting you right now?"

She dropped her head and said, "I can tell you, but it will make you mad."

"I can promise you it won't. I can handle whatever it is that you're feeling," I said.

Effie raised her head to meet my eyes and spoke to me directly. "I hate that you're writing a book. There, I said it."

I grabbed her hands and reassured her, "That doesn't make me mad. I think that it makes sense. You're used to me being around all the time. The time it takes me to write the book is time that is taken from you."

She started to cry. "Yes."

I pulled her in for a hug and just held her as she cried.

Let me ask you a question: How could I handle this situation so that no one was hurt?

I'll admit I went through a mental list of options.

- Could I write with the kids at home? I flashed to the yelling and screaming right outside my office door. Probably not.
- Could I go to the mountains too? Nope, same problem.
- What about not writing this weekend? Could I give up my time? No, I have so little time to spare.

So the question I had to answer in this moment was *Who was to be sacrificed, me or the kids?*

I chose the kids.

I don't choose their sacrifice often. In fact, my entire career and work decisions were constructed around being there for my future children. I wanted flexibility, time at home, the ability to be present and spend time with them while also having a career that brings me joy and fulfillment. I thought about this in college as I chose a path that would inevitably lead toward the necessity to obtain a graduate degree. I made life decisions based on prioritizing my future children.

But at this moment in my life, my work and my family were both high priorities.

The thing about all the commitments we hold in life—commitments to family, a partner, faith, community, work, health, friends, self (the list goes on and on)—is that they almost always exist simultaneously and often collide with one another, forcing us to choose. This is why we must learn *how* to commit wisely.

I will cover three defining aspects of commitment:

1. Promise
2. Perseverance
3. Priority

And then I will provide you with a scale to help you keep your commitments in check. The goal of committing wisely is having a sense of peace with how you arrange your commitments. The objective isn't to have some formulaic approach but rather to understand how to navigate the multiple decision points that arise day to day and moment to moment that require us to shift and organize our commitments. As you can tell from my story above, commitments often conflict, and we have to make decisions that feel hard, induce guilt, and can stir up feelings of tension as we try to juggle all the things when they *all* feel important.

## PROMISE

It was tuck-in time, and for whatever reason, I usually took the lead with Effie and Chad took the lead with Roy. This wasn't totally satisfactory for Roy, so he would finish up his dad tuck in and then yell from his bed "MOM" until I came in and drew superhero masks on his face and snuggled him. On this particular night, Chad had just returned from a weeklong trip, and I had been doing tuck ins solo, so Roy was feeling my impending absence. Before he entered his bedroom with Chad, he ran up to me and said, "You'll come in after, right?" "Yes, of course," I said. "Okay, pinky promise then." And he held out his tiny little finger.

That pinky promise meant serious business to him. It does to all kids really. It's the wimpier and much cuter version of a blood oath. I made a commitment to him, a promise, that I would show up in his room and be the closer for his tuck in. If I didn't show up like I said, I would have broken my promise.

When you make a commitment, you're making a promise. If you're married, you made a promise on your wedding day. When you sign up for a volunteer shift at the school carnival, you're making a commitment, a promise that you'll fulfill your shift. If you frequently break your commitments, you'll likely develop a reputation as flaky or unreliable. Or if you have to break your commitments with a particular person multiple times, even when it's out of character for you, you'll start to worry that you'll be perceived as flaky and unreliable.

Why? Well, the promise power of commitment is reinforced when your commitments are upheld. When you are someone who keeps your promises, people feel a greater confidence in you (aka higher trust) and that they can depend on you (aka higher reliance). When you break your promises, these feelings of confidence and dependability decrease.

Imagine if I told Roy that I would show up every night at the end of tuck in but then only did it occasionally. Sometimes I'd be there, sometimes I wouldn't. What would happen? Well, I predict that Roy would start to become anxious when Chad would leave. He would worry in his bed about whether tonight would be a night I'd show or not show. He would feel insecure in my promise to him. My promise would mean nothing.

Now think about how you make promises to yourself.

- From now on, I will wake up early for time alone.
- I will cut off that friend who makes me feel like crap.
- I will pray or meditate every day.
- I will stop scrolling and look my kids in the eye.

We make and break promises to ourselves all the time.

Just like in other relationships, broken promises lead to less trust and lower perceived reliability. This means that kept and broken promises to ourselves greatly impact our self-concept (see chapter 5) and how reliable we perceive ourselves to be (see chapter 6).

But what about flexibility? Ah, I hear you. We have to be flexible. What about the power of saying no? Sometimes self-care is canceling a commitment. I can see the Instagram posts in my head affirming your right to break promises for your own self-care. Sometimes this is necessary, and we will get to that.

Committing wisely doesn't mean you never cancel plans or prioritize your self-care; it isn't formulaic. There isn't one way. Rather, committing wisely is about feeling at peace with the way that you arrange and live out your commitments throughout the many decision points of your day. This may mean only making promises that you can keep. This may also mean reevaluating promises when it serves your own sanity but doesn't sacrifice your self-concept.

## PERSEVERANCE

The promise part of commitment is the vow or the statement that you will do something; however, carrying that promise out is what this second feature of commitment is all about. This is the grit of commitment. This is what helps you keep your promise even when it's hard or feels terrible. In marriage, the "for better or for worse" clause in wedding vows taps into this part of commitment. It's showing up to the gym even when you don't want to or pushing to meet that work deadline when you're totally crispy. This aspect of commitment is more complex than it seems on the surface and can help you understand why you are just toast at bedtime and how you can better follow through on your promises to others (which I bet is less of a problem) and to yourself.

When Roy started kindergarten, we noticed a marked shift in his behavior. He was like a stranger living under our roof—a really loud, cranky, agitated stranger. He was so dramatically different from the Roy from summer that I reached out to his teacher to make sure all was well on that front. She said, "Oh, Roy is a pleasure to have in class. He's making friends, he's very quiet, but he's doing great."

I was snuggling him one night when he looked at me and he said, "Hey, Mom. Did you know I'm the best-behaved kid in the class?" Ah, there it was. How did I miss it? Roy was struggling with this transition to kindergarten in a very specific way. He was holding it together all day at school and letting it all hang out when he got home.

This is the same reason why kids usually keep it together when they're with a sitter but then fall apart when they're with you. It's actually a psychological concept that is called different things like ego depletion, self-control, self-regulation, or willpower, and understanding this concept will help you parent your kids differently and mother yourself better.

There was a groundbreaking study done in 1998 by Roy Baumeister out of Case Western Reserve University in Ohio called the radish-chocolate study.[1] The experiment consisted of three groups: a no-food group, a radish group, and a chocolate and candy group. The no-food group went right to the final step of the experiment, which was a problem-solving task.

So let's focus on the two food groups. The researchers brought these participants into a room where they had just baked chocolate chip cookies. Upon entering they found a bowl filled with cookies and candies and another bowl filled with red-and-white radishes. For these two groups, it didn't end there; they were also told they'd be evaluated the next day and weren't allowed to eat any of these foods after the experiment. So if you had radishes in the experiment but were now craving chocolate, you were asked not to indulge your craving for twenty-four hours. Torture.

After eating either radishes or chocolate, the participants sat for fifteen minutes and then were asked to participate in a problem-solving task for thirty minutes or until they solved the problem. Unbeknownst to the participants, the task was impossible—literally an unsolvable problem. The experimenters timed the participants as they worked on the task, and here's what they found. Those who were in the chocolate group worked on the task for more than two times as long as the radish group. And those in the no-food group attempted to solve the task for more than two and a half times as long as the radish group. The chocolate and no-food groups persevered longer than the radish group.

Here is the key takeaway from this study, which also explains Roy's behavior on a much deeper level: *the more you exert self-control, the less of it you will have to use later.*

This finding was unique in that it explained a psychological concept in terms of energy. Thinking of this in terms of energy makes so much sense when applied to your life. Researchers, of course, needed a fancier bit of jargon and called the concept ego-depletion. But self-control, self-regulation, energy usage, or exerting your willpower all mean the same thing. For the purpose of consistency, I'm going to call this willpower.

The willpower these participants used to resist the chocolate depleted their resources. When they were asked to try to solve a difficult task, they gave up quicker. They made fewer attempts. When Roy spent all day being the best-behaved student, he used up a significant amount of willpower at kindergarten. When he got home, he was tapped out. He had no willpower left to exercise self-control. He was depleted.

Over the years many more studies have been done on this concept, and we know that our energy is also used up by many things:

- impulse control
- navigating unfamiliar circumstances
- delaying gratification
- controlling our emotions
- making decisions
- planning things
- self-criticism

- taking initiative
- executing plans
- temptation
- cognitive dissonance, which is doing something that's misaligned with what you believe
- low blood sugar
- lack of sleep

This list isn't exhaustive, but as you look through it, I hope you can begin to feel some compassion for your children and yourself.

Here are some key components to understand about how willpower works:

- Each of us has a different amount of willpower.
- Our willpower is limited each day.
- Willpower can be strengthened much like a muscle.

If you think of willpower like a battery, you begin each day fully charged. That is, unless you're a mom who is getting less than seven hours of sleep, which you probably are, and that means you're starting the day off with less willpower than if you were getting a full night's rest.[2]

Throughout your day you're engaging in things that drain your battery:

- Getting your kids out of the house
- Sitting in traffic
- Not going off on your boss
- Changing a squirmy baby's diaper
- Keeping it together during a tantrum
- Managing hurt from your teen's words or attitude
- And hello, mental load (one of the biggest willpower drains)

I could go on indefinitely. Throughout the day, these various things drain your willpower battery. This is why when you reach the end of your day, you may struggle to barely make it through tuck in. You're desperate to recharge. This is why you may be cheery in the morning and then lose it midday to late afternoon. You've used up your battery and likely didn't do a whole lot to reset throughout the day.

I hope so desperately that this is an aha moment for you. That you read this and go, "Oh my gosh, I'm not a terrible mother; I'm just out of willpower."

Okay, so let's bring this back to commitment and promises. Your willpower is what helps you to live out your promises. However, when your willpower is depleted and not replenished in the ways that are important and helpful, you will be less likely to keep your promises. You will simply be tapped out. Just like those participants in the chocolate-radish study, you will give up quicker.

To reiterate what I stated above, the risk in not keeping promises is that it starts to erode your trust in yourself, and your self-concept starts to change. This can easily translate into negative self-talk, which, guess what, uses up willpower.

It goes something like this:

- PROMISE: I am making a promise to nourish my body throughout the day. I cannot survive on dried-up mac and cheese and cold chicken nuggets.
- WILLPOWER USAGE: Your oldest had a bad dream, and you were up from two to three o'clock in the morning. Then you were running late for school drop-off because of unexpected traffic. You came home and found that your dog pooped on the floor and, of course, you stepped in it. You realize that you forgot to send an important email, and you rush to turn on your computer, only to realize your charging cord isn't there,

so you spend the next twenty minutes looking for it. You sit down sweaty and aggravated, and it's only 9 a.m.

- POSSIBLE BEHAVIOR: You run to the cupboard and throw some chocolates into your mouth.
- POSSIBLE SELF-TALK: *I can't believe I blew it today. I promised to nourish my body better, but it's not even noon and I already broke my promise. I suck. I can't stick with anything. I have no self-control.*
- TAKEAWAY: No one reading this would judge this behavior in others (admittedly, I've sought refuge before in the pantry and tossed back some chocolate-covered almonds); however, it's likely you'd judge yourself. Unfortunately, negative self-talk weakens willpower even further and starts to alter your belief in yourself.

But now that you understand how willpower works, you can approach this differently. You can:

- HAVE SELF-COMPASSION FOR THE TIMES WHEN YOU BREAK PROMISES. When you've used up all your willpower, you're bound to struggle with impulse control, emotional regulation, perseverance, and so much more (research says so).
- USE INSIGHT TO CHOOSE DIFFERENTLY. When you understand the process of how your willpower battery gets drained, you can face the situations with empowerment. You can
  - objectively call out what has drained your battery and choose whether or not you are going to engage in the impulsive act;
  - choose to recharge (more on this to come);
  - choose to pause, slow your decision-making, and be more intentional; or
  - sketch your trust picture differently and ultimately talk to yourself with greater kindness and understanding.

Here is the beautiful piece about willpower: it is like a muscle. You can strengthen it. When you break promises, you'll likely deplete or weaken your willpower. But as you keep them, you will begin to strengthen your willpower over time.

Here are some ways that your willpower can be strengthened:

- INCREASE SELF-AWARENESS. I briefly covered this above and in greater detail in chapter 4. Personal insight is empowering. Self-awareness assists in breaking down your decisions and choices into things that you can see and ultimately control. It raises issues to your conscious level so you can look at them and go, *Hmm, I see what's going on here. I don't want to do this anymore* or *This is working for me today.* It's adding intention behind the action. This is why so many dieticians recommend a food diary; it increases self-awareness about something specific: what you're eating. And then you can see it plainly and make choices accordingly.
- MEDITATE. This feels like a tired suggestion, but it really, really helps. Research has shown time and again that meditation has immediate as well as cumulative positive effects. Studies have shown that ten minutes of meditation a day can start to change the thickness of your prefrontal cortex, the area of your brain that's related to attention and control.[3] It works. Just start. Do it in small increments, and go from there. If you need help, there are countless apps, YouTube videos, and guided meditations to choose from.
- REMOVE WILLPOWER DEPLETERS. This is the simplest action you can take that will have an immediate impact. For example, if you struggle with being on your phone too much around your kids and this leads to you feeling guilt or self-judgment, then put your phone in a drawer for a designated time period. This can actually strengthen your willpower over time because each time you don't engage in the willpower

depleter, you experience a sensation of success or a "win." This is like a workout for your willpower, and with each success, it will grow stronger.

- TAKE CARE OF YOUR BODY. We will cover this in more depth in chapter 8, but eating well (your blood sugar levels impact willpower; for example, if your glucose is low, you will struggle with willpower), exercising, and getting adequate sleep impact your willpower in significant ways.

- SLOW DOWN YOUR HEART RATE (WHICH IS ALSO RELAXING). Studies have shown that willpower has a biological signature, which is heart rate variability.[4] Heart rate variability is just the time between heartbeats. The greater the time between heartbeats, the more self-control someone can exercise and the more relaxed this person will feel. Again, just to convince you, studies can predict whether someone will give in to temptation just based on their heart rate variability alone. Not surprisingly, exercise, meditation, and deep breathing all help to increase heart rate variability. A bonus effect is greater relaxation. And you can slow down your heart rate as you move through your day. Just breathe in and out slower and deeper.

Commitment is a promise that we make to others and ourselves. Keeping our promises requires perseverance through tapping into personal willpower. When we break our promises and this starts to impact how we see ourselves, our trust in ourselves declines, ultimately depleting our willpower even further. When we don't take time to recharge our willpower, we will have a harder time managing ourselves. We will have a harder time keeping our promises. We will have a harder time keeping it together. Part of keeping promises is having a strong willpower, and part of having a strong willpower is learning how to prioritize all our competing demands in ways that feel good to us.

## PRIORITIZE

Remember, the goal of committing wisely is to have a sense of peace with how you arrange your commitments. Part of finding that peace is being okay with how we prioritize. Maybe you prioritize eating that chocolate bar over the promise you made to eat healthy foods that day. If that's the case, there's a low chance you'll beat yourself up over that broken promise. In fact, I wouldn't even call it a broken promise; I'd call it a shuffling of priorities. And that's what this last section is about: how you prioritize your commitments in a way that results in peace and how you can cross-check the balance of your priorities so that you don't sacrifice all of you for the sake of others.

I opened this chapter by telling you about having to choose to sacrifice time with my family to write this book. I'm going to dive a bit deeper into this story, but there is an important takeaway that I want you to hear: *There is sometimes pain in prioritizing, primarily because you cannot prioritize one thing without de-prioritizing another.*

Life is a series of trade-offs. When you choose to do one thing, you are choosing *not* to do a whole bunch of other things.

> **You cannot prioritize one thing without de-prioritizing another.**

The reassuring piece to this is that it is impossible to prioritize all things at the same time. That's not a fair or even realistic expectation. The problem is that we act as if it *is* possible, and when we can't prioritize it *all* to the *same degree* and at the *same time*, we feel guilt and like we're falling short. Ahem, and this feeling of guilt drains your willpower.

I want to give you three primary tension points or trade-offs we're constantly juggling when it comes to prioritizing.

137

## 1. Urgent Demands Versus Higher-Order Priorities

Priorities are always in motion. At each decision point in your day, you choose what to prioritize. You can simply define a priority as where you spend your time. The tension in this area occurs when there is conflict between what we espouse to be our high-order priorities (family, partner, kids, work) and the urgent demands of life.

When Effie cried in my arms about being apart while I wrote this book, this was the tension I felt in my heart: my highest priority is my children and my family. Yet the urgency of my book deadline required that I choose to sacrifice my higher-order priority and hurt her feelings.

When moms feel the guilt about taking time alone, going on a girls' trip, or even just going to get their nails done, this tension is part of the story.

Here is the main takeaway from this first tension: *your higher-order priorities will regularly be at odds with your in-the-moment, urgent demands.* Sometimes you must sacrifice your higher-order priorities for the urgent demands of the moment (or even the season of life). This is normal. You would never wash a single dish, send a work email, shower, or make dinner if you didn't do this. I want you to know that this is necessary.

You may judge me for saying this, but I didn't feel guilty when I had to disappoint Effie to write my book. I felt sad. I missed my family. I hated missing out. But I didn't feel guilty. I know that this tension exists. I knew going into this process that I would make sacrifices, as would my family, and we decided, as a family, that the urgency of this opportunity would have to reign supreme for a while.

Take note that if you're feeling guilty about how you prioritize, you may be succumbing to the urgent demands more regularly and more often than prioritizing your higher-order values. This guilt may be productive in that it propels you to examine the distribution of your time and energy. If you say your family is the most important thing, yet you are always gone, never look up from your phone or computer, and use all your free time to pursue work, then it would make sense to reevaluate if family is *really* your higher-order priority. I know I've felt these productive pangs of guilt before when I have been with my kids but am really losing myself more in my phone. In these moments, my guilt acts as my conscience, reminding me to shift my energy in the moment.

The reassuring part is that priorities are always in motion. We get to choose how we arrange them in any given moment. When the kids got back from the mountains, I rearranged. I carved out special one-on-one time for each of them. We talked about what it was like being away from me, and I made sure to express how much I appreciated their sacrifice and how important it is for me to pursue something so deeply meaningful.

This tension isn't resolved by finding a perfect balance but by continually checking in on how you're balancing the two. And take heart: priorities can be rearranged in the moment, and you have the final say in their configuration.

## 2. Big Picture Versus Small Window

When I had to explain to Effie why I needed the time, part of my conversation was around how we need to commit wisely to things. We need to use discernment in how we arrange our priorities and that we sometimes have to commit to something now in order to be able to fulfill something else later. She got this concept and applied it to things in her life.

When I walked inside after comforting Effie to help Chad pack the rest of the stuff up, he said, "Well, it's hard on the kids because you've been gone a lot."

My insides were like an inferno. *"Gone a lot"? Say what?* Those words felt like a dagger to my heart. I have made decisions that make things more stressful for me in order to be there for our kids. We homeschool, and they spend three days on a homeschool campus and two days with me. Our kids are in grade school, and most grade-schoolers are gone five days! I'm with them *a lot* just given this difference in our schedule.

My husband travels weekly for work. I parent solo a significant amount of the time. My most defensive self wanted to shout, "Really?! I'm gone a lot; you're gone all the time."

Luckily, I had some decent willpower that day, and I kept myself regulated. Plus, I knew what he meant. You see, I had a friend in town the week before, and we went to the desert for three nights. So this meant that the kids were without me two weekends in a row.

Here's what had me defensive: this was so far from my normal routine with our family. In my nine years of being a mom, this was my first time going anywhere with a friend overnight. It just didn't happen. So to say I was gone a lot was a gross misrepresentation of the big-picture perspective of me as a mom. It was what I call a small-window perspective.

If someone had zoomed in on that part of my life, they may think that I was rarely around. Yet if they zoomed out, they'd see this was not the norm nor a trend; it was an outlier.

I highlight this tension because I am hoping it offers you relief and peace of mind.

I want to reassure you that if you are in a season of life that is abnormally busy, you may need to zoom out and look at the whole of you as a mother and the whole of how you prioritize and arrange your life. Try not to judge yourself based on a single episode but rather on what is the norm. Think about the overall trend of how you arrange your priorities as a mother versus all the other relationships, responsibilities, and routines in your life.

## *Arranging Your Priorities*

- **PEN YOURSELF IN VERSUS PENCIL YOURSELF IN.** Your other relationships and responsibilities will take as much time as you give them; make your time nonnegotiable.
- **DITCH SOMETHING THAT ISN'T ALL THAT IMPORTANT.** And substitute in time for you. We waste a lot of time on unimportant things; you're more deserving of meaningful attention than scrolling on Instagram.
- **SET A TIMER.** Set a timer for thirty minutes and spend it doing something that you truly enjoy.
- **MAKE USE OF DEAD TIME.** There are often moments in our day (ahem, school pickup line?) that we just default to picking up our phones and numbing out. Try substituting something in during that time that helps you feel rested or recharged instead of out of touch and mindless.
- **BOTH NEEDS ARE MET AT THE SAME TIME.** Sometimes there's an opportunity to find ways of meeting both your needs and your kids' needs at the same time, and this can open up opportunity for more time. For example, they watch a show and rest and you get to sit and drink tea in peace. See, both needs are met at the same time.

### 3. You Versus Everyone and Everything Else

This tension point is one that runs throughout this entire book. I spelled it out for you in chapter 1, and it will continue to be a major theme.

At any given moment of your day, you face a decision about how you arrange your priorities. Sometimes this happens with great stress and deliberation, sometimes it happens systematically, and sometimes it's automatic. No doubt there are pulls on your time and energy coming from responsibilities, routines, relationships, and likely your desire to rest, yet you can't do it all at once, and inevitably you will have to sacrifice some items on the list either temporarily or permanently.

Again, you can't prioritize one thing without de-prioritizing all the others. The problem arises when *you* are the thing that you de-prioritize time and time again. It's easiest to push yourself off the list of things to take care of. You tell yourself, *I've got this; I can keep going.*

Not really. Remember when we talked about willpower? It's a type of energy that runs out—you can't just keep going indefinitely without facing major consequences. Below is a continuum I want you to think about as you continue to shuffle your priorities. Use this picture to raise your in-the-moment awareness of how you prioritize you versus everything and everyone else.

## Balance of Priorities

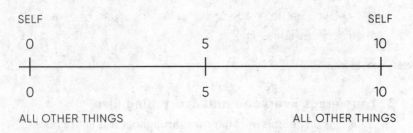

Let me explain. The balance of priorities between self and all the other things and people is like a seesaw. If you always prioritize all things above yourself, you will be heavy on the left side of the visual. Imagine yourself at the top of a seesaw, legs dangling, with all the other priorities of life firmly glued to the ground. If you neglect all your other priorities and focus solely on yourself, all your relationships, responsibilities, and more will be dangling up in the air.

The goal here isn't perfect balance but for you to have a way to visualize how you distribute your priorities and how you navigate this tension between yourself and everything and everyone else.

When you begin to feel burned-out, like your willpower is totally depleted, or you're feeling the pangs of resentment and being taken for granted, recall this visual. I would bet you've been de-prioritized; you're stuck on the top of the seesaw, and the weight of your responsibilities and relationship management is too heavy. You need to make a shift. You need to shuffle your priorities.

The goal of committing wisely is to arrange your priorities in a way that gives you peace of mind. This chapter isn't prescriptive; who am I to tell you what should take priority at any given moment of your day? I don't live your life. I don't have the same bank account, social support, belief system, values, partner, children, and life circumstances that you do. So committing wisely has to offer you flexibility within defined parameters. The parameter is the visual above; it's the seesaw of you versus everything and everyone else. It's you paying attention to signs that you're taking off and will soon be stuck at the top, weighed down by all the things you prioritized above your own care.

My wish for you in this chapter is that you raised your understanding of why you can feel so depleted in motherhood and that you gained permission to reevaluate how you prioritize yourself in the midst of all of the pulls of your priorities. I hope that you exhaled a giant breath of relief when you realized that you cannot prioritize all the things at the same time. And I hope you feel empowered that you have the agency to regularly shuffle your priorities, even in the moment, in a way that brings you more peace.

# *Go Mom Yourself*

### Step 4: Commit Wisely

- Make promises that you can keep.
- Have an awareness of your personal willpower capacity, and find ways to replenish yourself when you're running low.
- Be mindful of the distribution of how you prioritize yourself versus everyone and everything else. Use the Balance of Priorities visual to map out where you are on the seesaw.
- Ultimately, committing wisely is having peace of mind with how you navigate the competing demands that arise at the many decision points throughout your day.

SELF-CHECK-IN QUESTION: Am I a priority in my own life?

*Chapter Eight*

# STEP 5: TOUCH PURPOSEFULLY

In the early stages of writing this book, I was determined not to use the words *self-care* to describe what it was about. I attribute this to my countless hours spent on social media and seeing the barrage of information about the importance of self-care. I was sick of it. Also, *self-care* didn't feel like it was inclusive enough. This overused term wasn't enough to capture what I wanted to say in the entirety of this book; however, this chapter is the closest I'll get to talking about traditional self-care. You know, the "spa day, pedicure, go exercise, and eat a salad" self-care. This self-care has one thing in common: it is all about your physical self.

Our physical selves are just one part of who we are. We have our sensory self (know), our mental self (trust), our emotional self (rely), our volitional self (commit), and our physical self (touch). To just focus on the physical, like so much of the advice on this topic does, neglects these other aspects of the self. They work together and are *all* important to understand when it comes to nurturing our relationships with our children and ourselves. This chapter touches, no pun intended (JK, it was), on the last step of nurturing your relationship with yourself, and it is to touch purposefully.

There are three key areas regarding the importance of your physical self:

1. Stress
2. Sex and body image
3. Self-Support

After this chapter you will gain a new understanding and appreciation for the role that touch plays in your life and relationships, as well as understand how to touch purposefully in your relationship with yourself.

## THE IMPORTANCE OF TOUCH

In the late 1970s in Bogotá, Colombia, premature babies were dying at a rate as high as 70 percent. Two neonatologists were struggling with how to help these babies because they lacked the funding and resources to provide enough incubators for the newborns. Edgar Rey and Hector Martinez took inspiration from how kangaroos cared for their children and had mothers place their babies on their chests, bare skinned.[1] They then draped a blanket over mom and baby to mimic the pouch of a kangaroo. These babies thrived, and little did these two doctors know, they would forever change the way babies experience their first moments on earth.

The kangaroo method, or skin-to-skin contact, after a baby enters this world is now a common practice. This wasn't always the case; babies used to be whisked off to be bathed, clothed, poked, and prodded before being handed back to mom. Yet the evidence of the impact of this skin-to-skin touch was so undeniable that hospital policy changed.

Here are just some of the benefits of skin-to-skin contact:

## FOR THE BABY:

- Stabilization of body temperature, known as *thermoregulation*
- The transfer of good bacteria to establish gut health and prepare the baby for breastfeeding
- A reduction of crying
- Improved mother-baby communication
- Minimization of the experience of pain
- Improved weight gain
- More stable heartbeat and breathing
- Long-term benefits, such as improved brain development and function as well as parental attachment
- More success at breastfeeding immediately after birth
- A stronger immune system

## FOR THE MOM:

- A release of oxytocin, otherwise known as the "love hormone," which facilitates bonding and even the contraction of the uterus, reducing bleeding
- The baby gets to know her scent and can even crawl up to find the nipple and initiate breastfeeding (google it; it's so sweet to see)
- Higher breastfeeding rates and overall a more positive breastfeeding experience
- Improved breast milk production

- Likely to have reduced postpartum bleeding and a lower risk of postpartum depression[2]

Touch between a child and a parent, and a mother specifically, is mutually beneficial. Just like I discussed in chapter 2, our relationship with our children is not parasitic; it is mutualistic, and skin-to-skin contact is one more example of this. I hear you saying, "But what about when I feel 'touched out'? That doesn't feel mutualistic, lady." I get it, and I will get there later in this chapter.

Physical touch produces feelings of connection and comfort. When we are touched in ways that feel good, our body signals *I am safe*. This is what babies feel during kangaroo care. Think about our instinctual reaction when our kids come to us with a cut. We swoop them up, hold them tight, and kiss their boo-boo. We do this automatically; we intuitively know that touch is important.

The power of touch and what happens in its absence was never so drastically felt as it was during the COVID-19 pandemic. Some authors have coined the term *touch-hunger* to describe what was experienced by millions of people during the pandemic. Numerous studies connected touch-hunger to people experiencing an increase in aggressive behaviors, impairment in speech and communication, lowered self-esteem, increased anxiety, increased depression, increased self-injurious behaviors, and even eating disorders.[3]

While globally we've never before experienced this dramatic of a decrease in social and physical connection, we've known the impacts of touch deprivation for a long time. Harry Harlow was one of the first to examine the importance of touch and development in his series of experiments between 1957 and 1963. Harlow (1958) looked at how rhesus monkeys reacted when raised with inanimate "mothers" either covered in soft cloth or created from wire. Harlow found that the young monkeys clung to the cloth mother whether or not she provided food, but they only chose the wire mother if she provided food. Whenever something frightening was brought into the cage, the baby monkeys would cling to their cloth mother. In another experiment the monkeys were separated from their cloth mother for several days, and when reunited, the baby monkeys would cling to the cloth mother as opposed to exploring their environment. Again, touch signals, *I am safe*.

In contrast, the monkeys that were raised by wire mothers had difficulty digesting food and suffered from frequent digestive issues. Harlow concluded that contact comfort, or touch, is critical to the formation of a parent-child bond and that a lack of this contact is psychologically stressful. He also found that monkeys who were raised in complete social deprivation were severely psychologically disturbed. Harlow attempted to rehabilitate these isolated monkeys with very limited success and found that they had severe deficits in all social behaviors.[4]

This early research explained what we intuitively know, which is that touch is important in close relationships, especially among parents and children. Appropriate touch early in life provides a sense of safety, security, and love. Touch later in life also represents safety, security, and love.

Touch is also important in the relationship we have with ourselves. Our bodies require our care and love. The way that we nurture our physical selves, talk to ourselves, shape our perspectives, and manage our emotions all impact our physical bodies. In the book *The Body Keeps the Score*, Dr. Bessel van der Kolk, one of the world's foremost experts on trauma, described the ways difficult experiences reshape the brain and how the effects are then felt in the body. Medical professionals also have embraced the mind-body connection. For example, we now know that stressful emotions slow wound healing and alter white blood cell function, among many other things.[5]

Your body speaks to you, but are you listening?

Sometimes when you aren't in the know with yourself, when you don't have great self-awareness, your stress and strife come out in your health.

Sometimes when you see yourself as "less than" or when you compare yourself to others in a fruitless exercise of trying to level up only to feel like you're falling short, your body feels this exhaustion.

Sometimes when you are so focused on meeting the needs of others that your needs become back-burnered, you may start to feel the impact of your own self-neglect. Your physical body may bear the brunt.

Sometimes when you prioritize others so heavily that you ultimately neglect yourself, you might pay a major physical price.

We women in general, and mothers specifically, must learn to listen when our bodies are speaking to us.

Did you know that 80 percent (around 6.8 million) of people in the United States who have been diagnosed with autoimmune diseases are women?[6] And this is just the diagnosed. Autoimmune diseases are often complex and can take time and money to diagnose, so imagine how many women are living with undiagnosed autoimmune diseases. The question is why? There are three primary theories: (1) the X chromosome, of which females have two, offers a greater possibility of gene mutations; (2) hormones and the many shifts women go through, especially in pregnancy, may be linked; and (3) stress may be a trigger. Retrospective studies have found that, in up to 80 percent of participants, they could identify a stressful event that occurred just before the onset of their symptoms.[7]

We have got to listen to our physical bodies and touch them purposefully so we can feel fulfilled, rested, renewed, nurtured, loved, and safe. The rest of this chapter will help you to tune in to you. I will help you identify some of the greatest sources of impact on our physical bodies and what you can do about those things so you can expand your definition of care for yourself beyond a mani-pedi. However, if that's your jam, then by all means, go for it. And if you need something beyond the spa, I've got you too.

## STRESSED-OUT AND BURNED-OUT

I realize that it may be tempting to just skip right through this section. I mean, you know what stress is, you live it, and you probably throw this word around all the time. Who isn't stressed-out these days? But I challenge you to hang in there with me because I want to give you a quick, and hopefully entertaining, lesson on stress and burnout. Then I'll offer you some tangible things you can do to help mitigate the stress in your life.

Quick question: When was the last time you were stressed-out?

Follow-up: Where did you feel the stress in your body?

These two questions differentiate an important aspect of stress, and that is separating the stress from the stressor. Stressors are the events or situations that cause you to feel stress, while stress is the actual physiological reaction your body has to a stressor. This is really important to understand when it comes to dealing with your physical body and how it is impacted by stress.

One day when our daughter, Effie, was in second grade, she hopped in the car after school and appeared visibly stressed. She told me she felt scared after hearing a story from a boy at school. "Do you want to share it with me?" I asked. "Yes," she said.

Her voice sped up and her tone was panicked, but she went on to retell the tale. "So, there's this boy at school, and yesterday he was looking for gum in his mom's purse, and he accidentally sprayed himself with pepper spray."

I responded with "Oh, man. That is such a bummer. Is he okay?"

"Yeah, he's fine. He just told the class because he thought it was funny. He said he just coughed a lot. But now my stomach hurts, and I can't stop thinking about what if I get sprayed with pepper spray."

This worry stayed with Effie for weeks. When she would think about it, her stomach would ache, her palms would sweat, and her heart would pound. This was her stress response to the stressor: the pepper-spray story.

The wild part of all this is that Effie didn't even know what pepper spray was or what it looked like. If Sergeant Pepper Spray rang our doorbell and asked to come inside, she wouldn't even know she was talking to her biggest fear. Effie had never seen a bottle of pepper spray, we've never owned any since she's been alive, and there is virtually zero threat of her getting sprayed with pepper spray. But the physiological stress of the pepper spray was 100 percent real.

This is the downside of stress. We don't feel stress only if we're being chased by a lion in the Serengeti; instead, we are capable of imagining stressful hypothetical situations, and our bodies actually react to hypothetical stressors. These events don't have to occur, yet our body responds. It prepares us for fight, flight, or freeze.

Knowing that our body reacts to both real and imagined stress is key for understanding how we reach the point of burnout. We don't just reserve this intense stress response for life-or-death situations; instead, it is activated in us regularly, even if we only imagine potential scenarios.

Since I don't want to leave you hanging, I want to reassure you that Effie is okay. She moved past her stress around the pepper spray. I do have a confession, though. I didn't have the heart to tell her that when I was twenty-seven I sprayed myself in the eyes with pepper spray, and it was terrible.

The key takeaway from this section is that your body reacts to real and imagined stressors in the same way, by mounting a physiological response.

## STRESS RESPONSES

When our bodies react to a stressor with a stress response, they ready themselves to engage by setting off three possible physiological responses: (1) fight, (2) flight, or (3) freeze. Specifically, our amygdala detects a threat, adrenaline surges, cytokines are released, and the hypothalamus activates the release of the hormone cortisol. If you've read anything about adrenal fatigue, a common issue among women, you'll know how this stress response impacts our health and well-being. Your body's message is essentially *I am unsafe*, and it prepares physically by increasing your heart rate, sweat production, and blood flow to your limbs, slowing your digestion (you don't want to take a pit stop when being chased by a lion), and gearing up your immune system in case of injury. Essentially, your body produces a whole lot of "stress juice" to get you ready for whatever stressor is headed your way.[8] If you don't discharge the juice, you marinate in it.

In the book *Burnout* by Emily and Amelia Nagoski, the authors described the stress response as having a beginning, middle, and end. The gist is that the body is activated, the "stress juice" is released, and then it is *moved through* the body or discharged. They ingeniously coined the phrase "completing the stress cycle." Burnout occurs, as defined in their book, when you get stuck in the middle of the stress response.[9]

Let me give you some quick real-life examples that might clarify this concept.

- A dog shaking after a close encounter with a bigger dog: this is completing the cycle.
- A child punching a pillow or having a massive tantrum and then collapsing in exhaustion: they just moved the stress juice through their body.
- A primal scream in the car after facing a hard moment with your boss: this is discharging your stress.

Fortunately, modern-day life doesn't present the same life-or-death stressors as, say, life on the savanna. Unfortunately, we face many hypothetical and imagined stressors in which we have to interrupt the stress cycle while smack-dab in the middle.

Just think about all the times during the day when you feel stressed parenting your children. Or consider that moment when you want to tell your boss off, but you know you'll lose your job, so you swallow your anger. It is often considered impolite, inappropriate, or downright abusive to move through the stress cycle in various situations. The result is that we interrupt the cycle and move into our next stressful situation. We aren't closing loops; we are riding from stress response to stress response like a surfer on the waves. So on we go, marinating in that "stress juice," and wondering why we feel burned-out and physically ill.

## WHAT'S THE ANSWER?

When it comes to stress, there are many ways to manage it effectively. This entire book is geared toward helping you avoid burnout, so all the techniques suggested throughout the chapters thus far will help you to approach your stress differently and manage it more successfully. However, I hope that this is a book you will refer back to when you experience a new stage of motherhood or when a life event throws you off, so I want to summarize some of the most effective ways to manage stress right here in this handy section.

### Four Ways to Effectively Manage Stress

#### 1. CHARGE AND DISCHARGE

In chapter 7 I wrote about willpower and how regulating ourselves throughout the day uses up willpower. Part of dealing with stress better is not allowing ourselves to get to a place where we've used up all our willpower and our batteries are completely depleted. Incremental deposits into our battery can help to minimize our own meltdowns and offer protective effects against stress. And hitting the pressure release valve can also help to mitigate burnout and stress. In order to protect against the effects of stress, you must learn how to both charge and discharge effectively.

Here is a list of some of the most efficient ways—at least according to research—to charge and discharge; however, please know that you must tune in to you and determine what works best.

- GO TO SLEEP. Research suggests that about 42 percent of your day should be spent resting, and this includes sleep time.[10] I know, I know. If you're in the throes of newborn mothering, you have a toddler going through a sleep regression, or your kid has nightmares, you're likely reading this and rolling your eyes (or maybe rubbing your eyes). I know sleep sounds obviously necessary. But trust me, it really, really is. Sleep is essential because your body heals while you sleep. You integrate new information and skills when you sleep. You are less vulnerable to injury and sickness when you sleep. You handle your emotions better when you sleep. This isn't talked about much, but sleep can actually help to discharge stress. My husband is one of these unicorns who get tired when stressed and wake up refreshed and brand-new. If you're like this, you can be reassured that this is a real tool you can put to use. Pay attention to your sleep patterns, and track how many hours you sleep and how well you sleep. Play around with your bedtime. Can you make adjustments to improve your sleep hygiene?
- MOVE YOUR BODY. I cannot tell you how many times I've salvaged a terrible morning by cranking up some music and dancing it out with the kids. Exercise, dance, stomping, and shaking all help to discharge the "stress juice" from your body.

Exercise is one of the most recommended interventions for stress for a reason. It works. It doesn't matter how you move; just move your body! If you're interested, I have a free Spotify playlist, curated by moms for moms, to crank up during stressful moments so you can move your body and feel like you're doing it with a community of moms. You can find the playlist on Spotify under "Go Mom Yourself."

- EMOTE. When Effie is frustrated, she grunts really loudly. And when she's really upset, she screams into her pillow. I'll admit, I've let out a monster scream from time to time in my parked car or in my house alone. A loud scream or a good cry can do wonders for discharging stress. A cry that is ruminative can backfire, but a cry that ends with a big exhale and release is a great way to discharge.

- LAUGH OUT LOUD. Have you ever been stressed while you're laughing? I'm not talking about a frantic crazy laugh, but a really good belly laugh. It's nearly impossible. Laughter is an immediate stress reducer. It lets your body know, *I am safe.* Turn on stand-up or listen to a comedy channel on Spotify or Pandora or share a good laugh with one of your loved ones.

- CREATE SOMETHING. Are you old enough to remember the trending adult coloring books, or did I just age myself? You can still find them at craft-supply stores—those intricate drawings for adults to practice coloring in the lines. Why? Well, coloring is relaxing. Creating can be a major source of recharging and discharging. Throughout COVID, the kids and I did tons of art projects. I pulled up a stool alongside them, got out the watercolors, and went to town. It was the most relaxing practice I've done in years. Research shows that art therapy helps reduce cortisol levels, activate a state of flow, and distract a ruminative mind.[11]

- CARE FOR YOU. For some reason, plucking my eyebrow hairs feels relaxing. Perhaps this is why I looked like I had two tadpoles swimming across my face in high school. Thank goodness I've learned to keep this habit in check. Grooming and self-care rituals can help to charge your battery and discharge your stress. As promised, here is the typical self-care section. Think about what works for you. Maybe it's the spa, getting your nails done, a sheet mask, a Theragun, rubbing lotion on your hands at night, a gua sha, dry brushing, and so on. Tune in to you and think about the ways that you touch your body that feel good and recharging. Now do more of it.

## 2. CONCEPTUALIZE STRESS DIFFERENTLY

When I was preparing a presentation on stress and burnout for a company I occasionally work with, I came across Kelly McGonigal's TED Talk "How to Make Stress Your Friend." She had an interesting take on stress, which led me to read some of the research articles she mentioned and several more. Her thesis was "How we *think* about stress makes a difference on how stress affects our bodies."[12] There have been several studies that have supported her thesis, and here is the gist.

The belief that stress negatively impacts your health, combined with high levels of stress, actually predicts an increased risk of premature death. So experiencing a lot of stress and believing that stress is bad increased premature death risk by 43 percent. The same relationship was *not* found for people with only a high level of stress or a negative belief about stress.[13]

The same phenomenon was examined in a laboratory experiment, and the researchers found that those who were taught to believe stress was adaptive and helpful had a healthier physiological response to the stressor. Specifically, they had higher cardiac efficiency and lower vascular resistance, meaning less stress on their hearts.[14]

What this means is that the way that you think about stress

and its impact on your health and in your life makes a major difference in the way that it impacts you. You have the personal power to change how stress impacts you just by changing your thoughts about stress.

This is a win-win for busy moms like us. You don't have to add anything extra to your day besides shifting your self-talk, and it sounds like this: *I'm stressed right now, and this is just my body preparing me to handle what is on my plate. It isn't bad for me; it's my body doing its job.*

## 3. CONNECT

We are not meant to mother alone, yet so much of the time, that's what we end up doing. I've sat with friends before and fantasized about the days when moms worked together in a village and would all be washing clothes in the river, gossiping and existing in solidarity. I realize that this fantasy lacks some serious awareness of the realities of that life, like no running water or indoor plumbing, no dishwashers or cars or dryers or things that have made our lives arguably easier and more efficient. But the idea of living our day-to-day lives alongside other mothers who are experiencing the same struggles and joys of motherhood sounds refreshing. Because sometimes motherhood feels really lonely.

Rates on loneliness among mothers are hard to come by, but one study by Action for Children found that 52 percent of new parents felt lonely and socially isolated.[15] I would guess the rate is actually much higher. High rates of loneliness make sense, given that we live in a mobile and busy society. Perhaps you've moved and now don't have access to your family support network or you work and don't have the extra hours to devote to building community; you're just trying to keep all the balls in the air. I get it. However, a fundamental truth of life is that we are wired to connect. Connection is a biological drive and a physical need. Relationships with others play an important role in our mental, emotional, spiritual, and physical health.[16]

When you take a moment to tune in to you, when you are able to check in and notice that stress, ask yourself how you can connect to others. It doesn't have to be an event; just engaging in a quick venting session can be helpful. John Gottman, one of the world's more renowned relationship researchers, talked about the importance of the stress-reducing conversation, which is just a quick conversation in which someone shares their stressors with someone else. No fixing, no solving, just good old empathy.

Even a light conversation can fulfill this need for connection. When I moved to California, I will never forget my first trip to Trader Joe's. I had a one-year-old at the time and felt really isolated in my new home. I was far from most of my family and still getting my bearings. As I was checking out with my groceries, I was chatted up for ten minutes by the cashier. No joke—we covered my move to California, the law of attraction, and her excitement over a new relationship all while she bagged my groceries. This one brief encounter changed the trajectory of my day.

I've touched on this (there I go again with the puns) already, but physical touch is part of the stress-relieving process. Remember those monkeys and their cloth mother. Positive touch signals, *I am safe. I am okay.* Sometimes all we need is a twenty-second hug, which has been shown to reduce stress, to hold someone's hand, or to get a massage. Do not underestimate the powerful impact of physical touch.

### 4. CHALLENGE YOUR SELF-SABOTAGING STORY

You will notice that some of the concepts in this book start to reoccur. This concept was articulated both in chapters 5 and 6 and now again here. I will integrate them all for you in chapter 9, which is your reference chapter for quickly being able to grab on to these concepts and implement them in your life. With that being said, this will be a quick tip. In order to do all the things mentioned above to mitigate the effects of stress, you have to make time and devote energy to doing it. Sometimes we don't do this because we tell ourselves stories that sabotage our care.

Let me know if these sound familiar:

- There's never enough time.
- No one else offers me a break.
- I have too much to do.
- I don't deserve a break.
- If I take a break, I'm being selfish.
- It's too complicated or too much work to figure out how to get a break.
- It won't do any good anyway.

If these stories sound familiar, you've got to challenge them. They will prohibit you from nurturing yourself in the ways that you need. If you need to, go back to chapter 6 and complete the exercise to challenge these stories.

## SEX AND BODY IMAGE

### Touched-Out and Tapped Out

Most of us moms at the end of a long day with the kids have had the sensation of our skin crawling at the hint of more touching, let alone intimacy or sex. Being "touched-out" is a normal experience for moms. It intuitively makes sense, and most moms will nod in agreement if you mention feeling touched-out. It's almost a complete saturation of providing the love, comfort, affection, nutrition (if you're breastfeeding), and care for littles that can start to feel overwhelming.

Feeling touched-out is just one way we can become sensory overloaded. You can feel this same sensation in regard to noise, light, and other types of sensory experiences. They can also compound. If you've been touched all day and the kids have been especially noisy, you're likely going to reach this overloaded place earlier. If, on top of it, you are a *highly sensitive person*, you may be even more tuned in to some of these sensory challenges.[17]

Try to recall the way I described willpower in chapter 7 and all the things that drain it. One of the areas that drains willpower is sensory input. This is why you're likely touched-out or may be more likely to snap by the end of the day. This is why, by the end of the day, you're likely desperate for a break. Your power has been zapped, and your senses are overloaded. Touching at this point feels like one more demand.

The solution to being touched-out is often to touch purposefully—to care for your physical self in ways that help you to recharge and reset. Here are a couple of good options that can be done quickly in the moment:

- DEEP-PRESSURE TOUCH: This technique is used with people who have sensory processing disorders like autism but can also be a wonderful way to regulate yourself in the moment. You can try pushing your palms together firmly, dry brushing your skin, or even squeezing your hands into fists.
- A FIRM HUG: This can help to regulate your nervous system and also helps with relaxation.
- SLOW AND STEADY BREATHING: Work to slow your heart rate down, which increases willpower. You can do this by just stretching out your breaths as you inhale and exhale.

## Body Image

This section deserves an entire book. I'm asking you, in advance, for grace in this section, as there is just no way to cover it all. Yet I could not leave this topic out. Our bodies and the changes that they go through after having children is a huge part of our motherhood experience. Our bodies are a physical, tangible, visible reminder that we are not the same as we were before becoming mothers. I remember talking to my sister, Jess, over a year after giving birth, and I said, "It's so strange; it's like my rib cage is wider." Turns out, it wasn't my imagination because rib cage widening is actually a thing after kids. I know, our bodies are crazy!

Part of the work in nurturing our physical bodies, in touching them purposefully, is embracing our whole selves. When our babies enter the world, we marvel over their perfect fingers, tiny toes, and cone-shaped heads. We hold them and caress them; we do not critique and criticize them. How is it that we can accept these tiny humans and their imperfections so completely yet not offer the same love to ourselves?

If you have a daughter, I'm sure you've thought about how you want to raise her with a positive body image. I'm guessing that you may have even had to address some of your own body-image issues in order not to pass them on to her. You're already doing some of this work.

I want you to have reverence for your body because it is an incredible, magical, and powerful gift. The way you talk to yourself about your body matters significantly. In a neuroscience experiment *Do Words Hurt?* two scientists monitored brain activity when people heard or even thought negative words. What they found was that negative words released stress- and anxiety-inducing hormones in the subjects.[18] This just makes sense; remember when I said in chapter 7 that negative self-talk and shame depletes willpower? Part of the reason why is because it increases stress and anxiety, which then requires more energy to manage. When you talk negatively about your body, even to yourself, you're hurting you.

My advice to you regarding your self-image is to speak to

your body gently and with kindness. I encourage you to touch your body in loving ways. Treat your body with the same wonder and awe that you show to your beautiful children.

> **Treat your body with the same wonder and awe that you show to your beautiful children.**

Try to imagine yourself as a newborn, then a child, a teen, a young adult, and you now. What would you have said to yourself about your body then? What do you remember being proud of when it came to your body? How fast you were? How high you could jump? The bruise on your knee? Now, what did you need to hear as you grew up that you didn't? Try to give this affirmation to yourself now. Speak life into your body. Touch it purposefully and in ways that feel good. Thank your body for all it does for you, and care for it with the same compassion you show your children.

Also, listen intently to your body. As moms, we tend to quiet the pains we have in order to keep carrying on. We shove them down, ignore them, and just charge forward. In order to touch your physical self purposefully and in ways that really make a difference, you must listen to your body when it speaks to you. Your body is miraculous and has good intentions. If something is hurting, aching, throbbing, bloating, or burning, you're receiving a clear message. It's time to seek out help and care for you.

## Sex

When I talk about relationships after kids, one of the most common topics that come up is sex. Usually it's one of two things: (1) "I've lost my desire" or (2) "I'm touched-out." This is not a marriage book. This is a book for moms and their relationship with themselves, so I am going to talk about sex in that context.

Here's what I'd like you to know: you must deal with your body-image concerns if you would like to have a healthy sex life.

Particularly because your body image plays a major role in sexual arousal and desire, meaning being in the mood.[19] If you're worried about what you look like when you're having sex, you will most definitely be distracted and have difficulty getting and staying aroused. Body-image worry does not promote a sexy state of mind.

The second thing I would like to say to you around sex is that you are a sexual being with a massive amount of power. You have sexual power. Now, you may not feel like you do because you are tired, your body doesn't feel recognizable, you haven't been romanced in way too long, or you feel disconnected in your relationship. I get it. I also know that for many women (not all) sex is viewed or even treated as something you do *for* your partner. As if sex is a chore or one more thing to tick off your never-ending list of to-dos. Like sex is an obligatory sacrifice you make in order to fulfill someone else's needs. And here you are again, sacrificing self for the service of your relationships.

I want to encourage you to approach sex differently. I want to encourage you to take radical ownership of your sexual life. I want to encourage you to give yourself permission for pleasure and to step into your personal sexual power.

My encouragement isn't to force you or convince you to spice up your sex life in your relationship for the sake of your partner. Rather, my hope for you is that you take this as permission to shift how you view sex and your relationship with sex.

I want you to allow yourself to reexamine the following:

- What you've learned about sex and how this impacts you today
- What sex means to you in the context of your relationship
- What sexual needs you have
- What really turns you on and turns you off

- What your sex life could look like if you took ownership over your pleasure and sexuality

Not to be cheesy, but in the words of John Mayer, your body is a wonderland. Get comfy with it, and get to know your sexual self. Not for anyone else, but for you! If you haven't been told to do this yet, I'm not just giving you permission—I'm strongly recommending it.

## SELF-SUPPORT

As I write this chapter, I'm in the midst of trying to figure out some physical issues of my own. When I was fifteen I was hospitalized for two months for an unknown reason, but my body developed acute respiratory distress syndrome, or ARDS. ARDS is the effect of some shock the body endures, and ultimately it results in a hyperimmune response in which the body starts attacking itself. I was intubated, put on a ventilator, and given massive amounts of steroids in hopes of saving my life. My lungs were scarring over, and I had about a quarter-size of healthy lung tissue remaining. Thankfully, the steroids eventually worked and stopped my immune response. To this day, I still don't know the cause of my ARDS. The doctors didn't seem to care to revisit the reasons why; they just wanted to save my life. And I'm grateful they did. However, I have always wondered why and what that experience did to my body. Surely the root cause had to have been significant, and what are the effects of all those medical interventions?

I will likely never know, but the scars on my ribs and chest serve as reminders that my body has endured some hardship and shown incredible resilience. I am grateful to be here. The reality, though, is that my body has never been the same since.

Let's just say that my body speaks loudly to me at times, and I'm doing my best to listen. I sometimes miss its stressed-out whispers and continue to push through. Eventually, my back or my stomach starts speaking quite loudly, and I know that I need to tune in to my physical needs.

When you think of self-supportive physical needs, know that these are the things we need to do to care for our physical selves. They are the responses to our body when it speaks to us.

When our newborn screams because of gas, we bicycle their legs, switch their positions, rub their tummies, or maybe give them gripe water. But we don't just stand by and do nothing. We listen and we respond.

Touching purposefully means doing the same for you. It means doing more than standing by and telling your body, *I'll get to you eventually*; rather, touching purposefully means *I'm here, and I'm listening. Tell me what you need.*

I could list all the things you could do to care for your physical self, but you've seen those lists, and I'm not sure they're personalized enough for your needs.

For me right now, I know I need an endocrinologist or a functional medicine doctor. You may just need a good old back rub or a long soak in the bathtub. You have to be the one to determine what it is that your physical self needs. My deepest desire for you is just that you listen and respond.

# *Go Mom Yourself*

## Step 5: Touch Purposefully

- Manage your stress in ways that are protective.
- Embrace your physical body, and nurture a healthy body image.
- Step into your sexual power.
- Listen to your body when it speaks to you, and respond in the ways you need.

SELF-CHECK-IN QUESTION: Am I caring for my physical body?

*part three*

# where do we go from here?

# *Chapter Nine*

## GO MOM YOURSELF

A specific day of motherhood will be forever imprinted in my memory. I call this day "poof at the park." Effie was just shy of three, and Roy was four months old. I was desperate to hang out with a friend whose kids were the same ages but had totally different temperaments from my kids. I packed up snacks, somehow managed to get us all dressed without any poop mishaps, and loaded up the behemoth stroller with the bassinet attachment. I was ready to socialize, and no one was going to stop me.

At the time I was struggling with Effie's frequent and ferocious meltdowns. Parenting her felt like Whac-A-Mole; I never knew when one of her tantrums would rear its head, causing me sheer and utter panic whenever I left the house with her. I couldn't predict her tantrums. They would occur over everything from a gentle breeze to a misplaced marker. I had been consuming parenting books like a madwoman, convinced there was a way to crack the code. I just knew I had to be missing something. If I read enough experts' opinions, I could solve these tantrums once and for all. So, the method of the moment was something I called a "poof jar." I don't even know where I read about this stupid strategy, but I traveled around those days with a pocket full of tiny poofs (you may call them pom-poms) and a glass jar (glass—dumb, right?) to put them in. When Effie did something helpful, kind, or just generally good, a poof went into the jar. When we had issues, a poof came out of the jar. When the jar was full, *poof*, she got a Popsicle.

We pulled up to the playground, and looking out at the rubber palace that promised me adult conversation and company, I was thrilled. Funny how playgrounds can take on an entirely new meaning as a mother. I unpacked the car, flicked open the stroller, strategically unbuckled Roy first, and placed him in the bassinet. Then I unbuckled Effie and grabbed her hand and squeezed it three times for *I love you*. "We did it; let's find our friends," I said to her.

It was all going smoothly, as most playdates do until they don't, and then Effie came over and started playing with the poof jar—the glass one! I told her she couldn't play with the jar and redirected her toward the vast array of play equipment she had to choose from. This didn't cut it. Looking back, I'm not even sure what set her off, but the situation escalated from zero to one hundred quickly. Effie started grabbing the poofs from the jar and throwing them in Roy's bassinet. He was just old enough to grab stuff and put it in his mouth, so my mind quickly leaped to him choking on a poof and me having to live with the fact that I basically killed one child by attempting to coax my other child to behave using craft supplies and Popsicles. I quickly started picking up the poofs, but the bassinet was refilling faster than I could manage. I had completely lost control of the situation, and Effie was now in full-blown meltdown mode because I was undoing her handiwork. I had to leave. I don't even remember what my friend's reaction was because I was blinded by the rush of anxiety, panic, and sheer embarrassment. I announced our departure as I tried to calmly lift a kicking, squirmy, screaming toddler and push the bassinet back to the car. I knew what waited for me ahead: the dreaded car seat.

I wish I had learned to wrestle alligators earlier in life because that skill set would have definitely helped me in my motherhood experience. Effie is athletic. She is as strong on the outside as she is on the inside, and those early toddler years hold many memories of me trying to gently, and then less gently, get her buckled into her car seat. It was a fight almost every single time. But when she was in meltdown mode, it was nearly impossible. There were times when Effie had her fit and I would have to sit in the car for forty-five minutes, waiting until she was calm enough to get in her seat. That day, I didn't want to wait. I needed to go home and hide from my embarrassment. I quickly calculated my best odds of success and popped her in the back seat, buckled Roy, collapsed the stroller, placed it in the trunk, shut all the doors, and then used the walk from the trunk to the back seat door to prepare my mind and heart for the battle that would ensue. Eventually, I got her buckled. I placed my head on the steering wheel just right so I wouldn't beep the horn, and then I cried. I cried so hard, I would classify it more as a sob. I sobbed. Even writing this brings tears to my eyes.

These moments and now these memories are actually quite painful. I share them with you in case you see a piece of yourself in them because I think that these experiences are really normal. But they still conjure up a tightness in my throat and a sick feeling in my stomach because the poof at the park day (and many others) was a time in my mothering experience when I felt so incredibly disconnected from myself and who I thought I'd be as a mom. I will come back to this.

In this chapter I am going to review the five steps so you know exactly how to put them into action, and I'm going to walk through my story so you can see how the steps work in a real-life example.

## POOF AT THE PARK: MY SELF-CHECK-IN

I've known about the concepts I've written about in this book for what feels like forever, yet I didn't get good at applying them to myself until several years into motherhood. If I were equipped that day at the park, my check-in would have looked like the Relationship Attachment Model (RAM) below. Please note: at that point in motherhood, I was pretty disconnected from myself. My check-in now would look entirely different because I've been living out these skills in my life for years. In this section, I'm going to walk you through my self-check-in so you can see exactly how this looks in a real-life scenario. I'll then explain what I needed to do to make minor and major adjustments in my relationship with myself.

### 1. Define my current experience on the RAM.

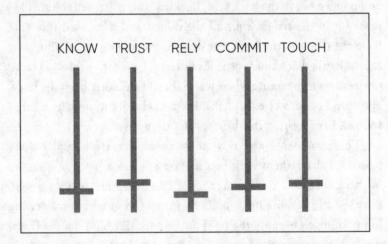

KNOW DEEPLY (AM I LIVING IN A WAY THAT IS
CONSISTENT WITH HOW I SEE MYSELF?)

A resounding *no*! I imagined I'd be calm, collected, and a heck of a lot less sweaty. I thought I would be an expert. I thought I would *never*—yes, never—lose my cool. I thought I would have kids who were chill. I thought I would be good at motherhood and that it would come easily. Most of all, I thought I would know what to do. Instead, I felt so lost. My knowing on the RAM was nearly at the bottom. I felt so misaligned and disconnected.

### TRUST ACCURATELY (DO I SEE MYSELF IN A POSITIVE LIGHT?)

No, not really. I was my own worst critic. As my husband, who's almost always succinct and matter-of-fact, would say to me, "You're too hard on yourself." Yes, I know. I was focused on all the ways I was falling short. My trust picture of myself was me weak, confused, lost, drowning, and inept. That was my focus. I held myself to impossible standards that I just couldn't meet. Things like *a good mom never cries in front of her kids, a good mom never loses her cool, a good mom wouldn't leave her kids to work, a good mom would know what to do in these situations, a good mom would have kids that behaved better than this*. I didn't like myself as a mom, and I felt so much guilt that it sucked the joy right out of motherhood.

### RELY BOLDLY (WHAT DO I NEED THE MOST?)

I didn't learn how to vocalize my needs clearly, assertively, and without the weight of guilt until several years into motherhood. I felt like I had to earn the right to advocate for my needs, and I didn't know how to do that. I felt like I would be imposing or asking too much. Also, I was so need deprived that I didn't even know where to start. If I asked for what I needed, what would I even ask for?

> **I felt like I had to earn the right to advocate for my needs.**

## COMMIT WISELY (AM I A
## PRIORITY IN MY OWN LIFE?)

My priorities at this time were almost all others and no self. I worked part-time from home, and I felt like that was my "me time." Even that was my boss's time, not my time. This was not time in which I felt refueled. There was another part of me that felt like since I wasn't with the kids while I worked (even though I was just in another room), I somehow had used up my self-inflicted quota of time apart from the kids. I couldn't take any more time away, especially time to meet my "selfish" needs for care. So I made my needs small and felt frustrated, resentful, and burned-out.

## TOUCH PURPOSEFULLY (AM I CARING
## FOR MY PHYSICAL BODY?)

At this time, I was not listening to my body. It was shouting at me in the form of lower-back pain, but I couldn't get past my other issues (asserting my needs, feeling like I could take time for me) to actually do anything about it. I had stopped exercising when Roy was born because it felt too hard with two kids, and I generally felt uncomfortable in my skin. My body was different, and it hurt, but I didn't do anything about it.

## 2. Determine where, when, and how I will realign.

My path back to myself was a long one because I had some major work to do. You may find yourself in the same position of needing to do work on each of the five steps. To give you a good example of how these steps work in both the long-term and in the moment, I will analyze the poof park day two ways: long-term work and in-the-moment adjustments.

## LONG-TERM ADJUSTMENTS

My major shifts occurred in two areas: trust and rely. I've said before that when you adjust one area, others are affected, so naturally as I worked on these two areas, they enhanced one another and eventually the other three bonds.

I started by examining my trust picture of myself. My focus was on all the ways I was falling short. Specifically, I had to challenge the conclusions I had drawn about myself and who I was as a mother. This wasn't as hard as I thought it would be. I took the time to write out my beliefs, and then I worked through the exercise of holding my beliefs up to my reality. If a friend came to me and said, "I think I use up my 'me-time quota' while working, so if I ask for time alone, I'm a bad mom," I would have been tempted to bop her on the head with the hope of knocking some sense into her. Why did I accept that as a truth in my own life? Why did I think this was true only for me? So I decided it wasn't, and I revised this standard.

When I examined the impossible standard of *a good mom has perfectly behaved kids*, I realized I had to cut the cord that tethered me to the belief that Effie's behavior was a direct reflection of my value and competency as a mother. I created a mantra for these moments: "Effie is having a hard time; that doesn't mean I'm a bad mom." This took so much pressure off. If her behavior didn't mean I was a bad mom, I had more space for empathy and compassion for her instead of being filled to the brim with self-loathing and shame.

I also adjusted the expectations I had for myself during Effie's tantrums from feeling like I needed to "fix" them to just having to be there for them and staying regulated. I always knew this, but in the storm of the tantrums, my anxiety and self-judgment were so loud, I lost hold of this truth. This adjustment alone took so much off my plate. No more reading. No more scouring the internet for days on end, sorting through mixed messages. I just employed tactics like slowing down my breath and repeating my mantra to help me stay regulated.

The second piece that I needed to work on was having the courage to assert my needs. I know how hard this can be. I have a partner who is supportive and doesn't give pushback, and I still had a hard time making this shift, so I know that varying degrees of resistance may come up when you assert your needs. Here's just a sample of some of my narratives around needs:

- I don't want to come off as needy.
- I am too much.
- I should be able to handle it all. I'm weak if I can't.
- I don't want to inconvenience anyone; we're all tired.
- I need to earn the right to advocate for my needs or even put them first.
- A good mom is needless.

I spent a great deal of time reflecting on these narratives. I connected them to messages I received growing up that I believe were well-intentioned, yet I was left with some different interpretation of them. I worked to adjust the conclusions based on what I know to be true when I take my emotion and anxiety out of the equation. I know that a good mom isn't needless. I know that I am not too much. I like how much I am. I know that I can't handle it all. No one is calling me weak except for me, and I can shut her up. No one but me is saying I need to earn the right to ask for my needs to be met. I decided to be done with those other beliefs, and I did two things.

1. I changed my internal narrative. Here's a sample.
   - *I am strong and vocal, which may be too much for some people, but I love those things about me.*
   - *I can't do this on my own, and I shouldn't have to. Asking for help is courageous.*
   - *I am not an inconvenience. I am the lifeblood of our family; I have to stay solid.*
   - *No one is judging me other than me, and I choose to stop doing that.*

- *All people have needs. I should know, as I'm meeting others' needs all day long.*
2. I changed my behavior before I felt totally ready.

Sometimes when it comes to making major changes in how you live your life, you have to act different before you feel different. Even better if you do both at the same time. I started acting as if I was the woman and mother I wanted to be before I felt like her. Here are some things I did.

- I joined a gym with childcare and didn't beat myself up for putting the kids in there for an hour. I was genuinely a better mom for working out some energy.
- I announced to my husband that I would be asserting my needs more. And then I did.
- I didn't ask for permission to go to the bathroom; I just went.
- I didn't ask for permission to take a shower; I just took it.
- I told my husband I couldn't keep up with all my responsibilities and the finances, so I turned that over to him. Best decision ever.
- I said things like "I need a break; what day is good for you to take the kids?" or "I really would like to take a walk; when's a good time?"

Basically, I stopped asking permission and started reclaiming my place as a member of my family who also had needs. This took time and practice and mechanical effort until it became second nature. But I haven't looked back. And I'll tell you what—I am a better wife, mother, and woman for it. It feels powerful and aligned.

Some small practices I've also engaged in have made a difference along the way. I'll share one with you that has been particularly helpful.

Before I mindlessly jump into a task like washing the dishes, straightening up a kid's room, or picking up LEGOs (yes, the kids do this, too, but you know sometimes you just want it done), I pause and ask myself, *Is this how I want to use this time?* Sometimes the answer is a resounding yes! Sometimes it's a no, and I sit my butt down and snuggle the kids or sit in silence. I regularly check in with how I'm prioritizing the moments of my day so that I do it in a way that feels good to me.

Remember I said that the five areas work together? Let me sum it all up: As I reflected and raised my self-awareness (know), I was able to outline the thoughts that sketched my trust picture (trust). This allowed me to challenge and resketch this picture (trust). When doing this, I also unearthed my expectations and standards around needs (rely). I revised these and began behaving differently, which helped me experience the empowerment I needed to prioritize myself differently in the landscape of my life (commit). And this ultimately led to me taking better care of my physical self in a number of ways, like exercising, going to the chiropractor, getting my blood drawn, and regularly having opportunities to de-stress and connect with others (touch). In the end, I felt more like the mom I thought I would be and, more importantly, more connected to myself.

## IN-THE-MOMENT ADJUSTMENTS

Let's say, for the example's sake, that I had already done all the work described above before heading into poof park day. I had put in the time to work through some of the bigger issues and was now just practicing those quicker self-check-ins. This is what it would have looked like in the moment, and I would have done my self-check-in during that walk from the back of the car to the side door, where I would greet Effie for the car seat battle.

## 1. Define my current experience on the RAM.

On the next page, you'll notice that I'm not in as rough of shape as I was in the other scenario. Why? Because I had already made

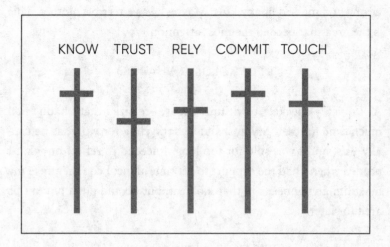

major shifts; now it was just a matter of recalibrating when life and circumstances, as they always do, pulled me away from myself.

Okay, so let's run through the five areas.

### KNOW DEEPLY (AM I LIVING IN A WAY THAT IS CONSISTENT WITH HOW I SEE MYSELF?)

In that *instant* I didn't feel like the mom I imagined myself to be, but *most of the time* I did. This is the shift; this is why the know level isn't tanked but instead just slightly lowered. Most of the time I was living in alignment with who I wanted to be and imagined myself to be, but in this circumstance I wasn't. Because this wasn't my typical state, I wouldn't beat myself up over it as much as I would have in the other scenario. I'd know, *This is a temporary glitch, not my typical mode of operation.*

### TRUST ACCURATELY (DO I SEE MYSELF IN A POSITIVE LIGHT?)

Trust took the biggest hit during poof at the park. Old narratives rose to the surface, and I started to feel like maybe they were right. Maybe I didn't know what I was doing. Maybe I had parented wrong and messed up my kids. Maybe I was a terrible mother. This is the area that needed the most attention.

### RELY BOLDLY (WHAT DO I NEED THE MOST?)

As I quickly checked in with my needs, I realized that I hadn't had much time to reset. My husband was traveling for work, as he usually was, and I was solo for too long. I needed to reflect on what I needed when I had the support to get time alone. I couldn't meet my most life-giving needs in that moment, but I could put a pin in this area for later.

### COMMIT WISELY (AM I A PRIORITY IN MY OWN LIFE?)

My priorities were imbalanced in part because of the logistics of my partner's travel schedule but also because I was living in mom survival mode. I wasn't paying attention to the multiple decision points in my day where I could care for me or do more. I needed to shift.

### TOUCH PURPOSEFULLY (AM I CARING FOR MY PHYSICAL BODY?)

I had been regulating a lot with Effie's tantrums, and my body was feeling tense and on edge. I hadn't discharged my stress, and I wasn't sleeping much because Roy was in the dreaded four-month sleep regression. My physical self felt off.

## 2. Determine where, when, and how I will realign.

My quick reset during the walk from the trunk to the side door would be targeted at trust. The other areas needed some adjustments, but in that moment, my most powerful go-to would be to change my focus and bring my mantra to the forefront.

I would take a deep breath and imagine rearranging my picture of myself. I would remember the mantra, "Effie is having a hard time; that doesn't mean I'm doing a bad job." I would say this over and over. I would focus on all the ways I show up for her and my family. I would take the focus off the tantrum. I would remind myself how I disconnected my worth from our kids' behavior.

It's worth noting that I also automatically resketched my picture of Effie. Let me explain. If I saw her in that moment as "difficult" or "bad," I would likely treat her differently than I would if I saw her as having a hard time. Remember when I said our relationships are mutualistic, meaning they work together? When I resketched my picture and brought my mantra forward, I also resketched my trust picture of Effie. We both benefitted.

As I rounded the corner of the car and put my hand on the door handle, I would tune in to my body quickly. I would reassure myself that I could handle what was to come and that I needed to pay extra attention to calming strategies. I would also reassure myself that when I got home, I would find a way to discharge my stress. Since I was solo with two kids, this might look like cranking up some music and having a dance party, but discharging was essential. Another point of reassurance would be that I would request time to regroup when my husband returned. In fact, I made the decision to tell him on the phone that night to think about a time when we could fit it in after he got home. This didn't meet my need immediately, but it felt good to know that help was on the way . . . dear, IYKYK.

Would I still have cried on the steering wheel when I got to the driver's seat? Maybe. I'm not really sure. But I can assure you that it wouldn't have been followed up with self-deprecating thoughts and a spiral into shame. I would have been equipped with a plan and would have felt congruent with who I thought myself to be as a mother. I wouldn't have carried the extra weight of managing the negative self-talk that would have undoubtedly worn down any willpower I still had left. I could have left poof at the park feeling equipped and at peace.

## CONCLUSION

The concepts and tools in this book are versatile. If imbalances have existed for a long time in your relationship with yourself, you can go deep, just like I needed to do. If you've done that work and you're in maintenance mode, you can quickly move through your self-check-in multiple times a day.

## *Remember Your Self-Check-Ins*

- Set a reminder on your phone to alert you once a day to tune in to you.
- Choose part of your daily routine and use it to trigger a reminder to check in with you:

  - When you go to the bathroom, instead of scrolling, do a check-in.
  - When you're breastfeeding, use this time to check in with you. Plus, it's safer than potentially dropping your phone on your baby's head.
  - Before school pickup, take a moment to check in with yourself before the massive transition.

# LOST AND FOUND

I have felt lost thousands of times in motherhood. Here's just a sampling; maybe you'll see yourself in one of these.

- When I wrestled Effie into her car seat too many times to count
- In the vulnerability I felt in our marriage after becoming a mom; I had "baggage" now
- The time I cried into a pile of laundry
- When my husband seemingly lived life just the way he always did, but my life had changed significantly; I felt left behind
- When I was up at night breastfeeding and lonely
- In the homesick feeling I experienced right after birth
- When I developed anxiety at nighttime, worrying whether I would get enough sleep
- When I saw my body in the mirror
- When I had nothing to talk to my husband about because I felt boring and like my life revolved around the kids
- When I had a really hard time figuring out how to schedule a haircut
- When I had a kid I didn't know how to handle

- When I was stressed, frazzled, grumpy, and sweating in public
- When I breastfed in a bathroom stall at the airport
- When I felt flustered by a child's restaurant meltdown and had to leave
- The time I left a full cart of groceries in the middle of an aisle because I couldn't contain a tantrum
- When I was bored playing on the floor with our kids
- When I cried in my closet or the pantry because it all felt like too much
- When I've looked at my kids and wondered how I will function when they're grown
- When I stormed off to my room for a break because I felt like I was suffocating
- When I had countless angry conversations in the shower about why no one thought of me
- During my first trip to the mall with a baby when I had to do three outfit changes because of diaper blowouts

I share these examples, and I could go on, because I want you to know that you will regularly lose yourself in motherhood and that it is totally normal. The last thing I want is for you to leave this book feeling guilty for the times you're "out of balance" or disconnected from yourself. Motherhood will do that to you—it does it to all of us. The key takeaway is that you can't stay that way forever without sacrificing yourself, your sanity, your health, and even the quality of your relationships with your kids and partner (if you have one).

Yes, you will become disconnected. But now you have a definition for what you're experiencing and a tool that will help you quickly assess the areas that need care the most. The judgment, shame, and guilt you feel when you aren't doing all the things that you worry you "should" be doing can dissolve away because you know how to adjust. And when you feel you're doing "too much" for you, you can find comfort in knowing that it won't be long before you're lost in your kids again. You have all that it takes to manage your relationship with yourself with confidence and hopefully a whole lot of self-compassion.

I want to leave you with some musings before we end our time together, and if you need to be reminded of these thoughts later on, you can simply flip back to the final chapter of this book and read my words to you.

*You are strong, and your strength lies within you.* Throughout this book is a message of tuning in to you. As women and mothers specifically, we are so dialed in to others and all that they need and require. I am proud of this quality in myself and have benefited from the women in my life who have shown up for me or intuited something I needed or cared for me. We're pretty spectacular in that way. I want to nudge you to be inwardly attentive more often and to use the same strength, wisdom, and caretaking that you possess as a mother and direct it toward you.

*This is not a solution; this is a practice.* I don't say this to crush your hopes of feeling better but to remind you once again that relationships with others and ourselves have an alternating rhythm; they have life to them. They move from connection to disconnection and back again. There is no final destination; rather, this is a practice for you to incorporate in your life to stay in touch with yourself and to help you evaluate where you need attention the most.

*Sometimes you won't have the time, but you will always be able to define.* Time is finite. If I had magical powers, I would grant you all more time, not so that you could get more done, but so you could have margin in your day to truly enjoy and relish doing nothing (or whatever brings you joy). There will be many times that you recognize you are disconnected from yourself and you just won't be able to get to it. Take heart that it's okay. Take comfort in knowing that defining your experience is freeing in so many ways. And know that if you can't do anything else, you can change the way you think about yourself and your circumstances (see chapter 5), and this will be helpful.

*Sometimes you will have to find peace in the storm, but storms don't last forever.* Seasons of motherhood differ in terms of the intensity of your children's needs and all the other things you have going on in your life. I know I've white-knuckled some seasons of motherhood when my husband was traveling a lot, we were renovating with two young children, or life's responsibilities were just colliding. During those seasons you may have to find ways of discovering peace in your storm. Many of the strategies in this book will help you with this. You may find that your go-to during these hard moments is using your anchor to ground you in yourself, adjusting your trust picture of yourself, defining what you need, slowing down your breath to increase willpower, or touching your body in ways that are soothing and meaningful. But know that there are tons of options for fitting in care that will sustain you until the storm passes.

*Your change at home can change the world.* Early in this book I made it clear this was a book about things you can do in your own life. This wasn't a sociological book about the patriarchy or societal oppression of women or mothers; this is a practical book about what you can control. However, I just want to call out this simple fact: the changes you make in your home have a ripple effect that can ultimately lead to dramatic and positive changes in society. This is a bottom-up approach to change. When you reposition yourself in the hierarchy of care and time in your family, when your partner (if you have one) and especially your kids experience you asserting your needs, prioritizing differently, seeing yourself in a positive light, and tuning in to your body, you will change. And they will change. You will feel at ease and surprisingly powerful because you've become unshackled from the debilitating messages that you didn't deserve to be nourished. Your children will learn that they, too, can be emboldened to care for others without forgoing themselves in ways that are meaningful and have depth. This change will fan out, impacting the norms and patterns of future generations, and it all starts at home with you. That's pretty amazing.

---

Mama, you are a giver and a master manager of all the things and all the people. My desire for you is to use the incredible skill sets you already have and turn them toward *you*.

I deeply wish for you to stop waiting for someone else to give you permission to nurture you. And instead of outsourcing your care, you lean into the personal power that you contain to rearrange how your needs, nourishment, and wellness are prioritized.

I want you to really let these next words soak in.

You are not needy.

You are not too much.

You are not required to give all of you in order for others to thrive.

You must not give all of you. In fact, it is imperative that you don't.

You deserve to live a life in which you feel at peace.

A life where you have less guilt and more lightness. Where you have less moments of soul-sucking burnout and more moments of joyful play and laughter. I want you to know that you have radical permission to take that last piece of cake, to eat dinner while it's hot, to go pee, to take a vacation without the kids, and to pursue something that brings a sparkle to your eye. There is room for you to wholly exist in your family.

My parting words to you are an invitation rather than an insult. They are words to pull you out of the waters when you're drowning. They are words to put a smile on your face when you know you just need to tune in to you. Ready for it? *Go mom yourself.*

Share this message with the mamas you know and love.

# DISCUSSION QUESTIONS

These questions are meant to prompt you to reflect on the concepts in this book. They are also meant to save you time and effort if you would like to do a book club or small group study. One idea is to choose one or two questions and discuss them with the other moms in your group. I hope you find them helpful and a time-saver. You've already got enough going on—you don't need to be writing discussion questions too!

## CHAPTER ONE: WE MOM SO HARD

1. What are some normal life events that throw you out of balance and result in you feeling more disconnected from yourself?
2. What are some subtle or unnoticed ways you sacrifice your needs for others in your life? When you do this, what feelings tend to rise up in you?
3. What ideals did you hold about motherhood? Talk to your friends or among the other moms to reality-check these ideals. Can you shift one ideal to be more in line with reality (and what other moms also experience)?

4. How does intensive parenting show up for you? Talk about the pressures you feel to be the "perfect" mom. Where do these pressures come from? Brainstorm ways you can set boundaries around these behaviors when they're causing difficulties. Hint: you can do behavioral things to reinforce these boundaries or even set mental boundaries.

## CHAPTER TWO: MOTHER YOURSELF
## LIKE YOU MOTHER YOUR KIDS

1. How does burnout show up for you? What are the early signs that you're headed in that direction?
2. What objections come up for you when you consider changing how you care for yourself? Can you identify a time when you cared for yourself well? If so, how did you feel different? How did you relate to your family differently?

## CHAPTER THREE: CREATE
## LASTING CONNECTION

1. Map your relationship with yourself on the Relationship Attachment Model (RAM). If you're in a group, each of you should take a moment to do this. Reflect on or discuss what you notice. Where do you see places for possible changes? How does your profile on the RAM reflect the way you're feeling right now?
2. If you have multiple levels that are low, which one feels most important for you to tackle first? Which one feels the most doable?
3. Choose one child and map your relationship with them. How do you think your relationship would change if you worked on your relationship with yourself?

## CHAPTER FOUR: STEP 1: KNOW DEEPLY

1. How was love shown in your family growing up? Were there any conditions to receiving love in your home? How do you see some of these early experiences with your family showing up in your life today? How are you changing or repeating these patterns with your own children?

2. How were emotions handled in your home growing up? What messages did you receive about what it means to have "big" emotions? How do you see some of these early experiences with your family showing up in your life today? How are you changing or repeating these patterns with your own children?

3. When you think of your mother, what did you learn about what it means to be a mother yourself? What did you learn about what a "good" mom should do? How did your observations and experiences shape your expectations for yourself today? (If you didn't grow up with a mother, think of a prominent female caregiver. Also consider that the absence of a mother is significant and gives you much to reflect on.)

## CHAPTER FIVE: STEP 2: TRUST ACCURATELY

1. Take a moment and draw your trust picture of yourself the last time you had a tough moment. If you're in a group, talk about your pictures together. Notice and reflect on what you're highlighting and focusing on and what you're minimizing. Do you notice in hard moments that you tend to focus in on the same negative things? How can you edit your picture to be more accurate?

2. What is the story you're telling yourself in these tough moments? How do the information you consume, societal messaging, and your early experiences play a part in shaping this story? Come

up with a one-line mantra to rewrite this story to be more accurate. If you're in a group, share your one-liners.

3. What "shoulds" do you regularly repeat to yourself about the type of mom or woman you should be? What impossible standards do you hold yourself to that have come out of these "shoulds"? If you're in a group, share (and hopefully laugh at) some of each other's impossible standards. Reality-check them together.

## CHAPTER SIX: STEP 3: RELY BOLDLY

1. When you think about making your needs known in relationships, how do you anticipate others will respond to you? Please note: you may have different answers for different relationships.

2. How does this anticipation of others' reactions impact your behavior around your needs and whether you express them? If you're in a group, discuss the similarities in your experiences. It's always nice to learn you're not alone.

3. What are some of the messages growing up that you received about needs? If your adult self could meet your child self, how would you mother her right now? What does she need to hear about her needs that maybe she didn't get growing up? If you have the energy for it, write your child self a letter of reassurance affirming her right to have needs and giving her permission to express them. Of course, add anything else you think would be helpful for her to hear.

4. What do you need in each of the categories of needs? Write down what you need and how you'd love for this need to be met. The categories are logistical, emotional, affirmational, purposeful and spiritual, and physical. If you're in a group, have each person pick one of the needs and brainstorm either (1) practical ways of expressing the need or (2) how to prioritize getting this need met in your life.

## CHAPTER SEVEN: STEP 4: COMMIT WISELY

1. What is a promise to yourself that you continue to make and break? Take this moment to determine whether you want to ditch this promise for now so that it doesn't drain your willpower or make a plan for how you can recommit and keep the promise to yourself.

2. Now that you understand the concept of willpower and what drains it, what are some of the biggest willpower depleters in your life? If you're in a group, discuss these together. Can you choose one and come up with a plan for how you can approach it differently so that you aren't so negatively impacted by it? Get creative with your ideas.

3. What are your higher-order priorities? Where in your life do these conflict with your urgent demands? As you reflect on this, does it seem like you are living in a way that values your higher-order priorities? If so, come up with a mantra to help you through those moments when you must justify leaning into the urgent demands. If not, how can you shift either your priorities or your life to be more in sync with one another?

4. Using the balance of priorities continuum on page 142, draw a dot where you are on the line right now. If you're too far in one direction, what would moving a little closer in the opposite direction look like for you? Brainstorm practical steps you could take to change the balance of your priorities.

## CHAPTER EIGHT: STEP 5: TOUCH PURPOSEFULLY

1. What are three things in your life that trigger a stress response? These can range from the totally minor (kids not putting their shoes on when you're running late for school) to the major (financial struggles). Use the list from the chapter, and brainstorm

small tweaks you can make to help discharge or manage that stress differently.

2.  When it comes to taking care of your physical body, what is your self-sabotaging story? If you're in a group, share your stories with each other; I would bet there's some overlap. Rewrite your story so that you aren't blocking your ability to nurture your physical self. If you're in a group, gather info from the others to help you rewrite this story. Outside opinions and thoughts go a long way toward challenging our stories.

3.  How is your relationship with your body? When you look at yourself, what words flow through your mind? Come up with one or two positive phrases you can say to yourself (out loud or inside your head) when you look at yourself in the mirror. As you start to practice this, notice if you feel similarly or differently about your body.

4.  Imagine that you were in your sexual power, and describe what that would look like. How would you dress, move, talk, and feel? What is one change you can make to take a step into your sexual power? Maybe you're not even in the same room as your sexual power, but if you took a step closer, what would that look like? What practically would you have to do?

5.  What type of physical care and touch feels good to your body? List some of the rituals or care that feel best for you. Brainstorm ways of increasing how often you incorporate these into your life. If you're in a group, use the other moms to crowdsource how they fit this care in.

# *A Deeper Dive*

## HOW TO KNOW
## YOURSELF DEEPLY

**U**se these reflection prompts and questions to help you begin to define how you see yourself, what's important to you, and what brings your life meaning.

## HOW DO I SEE MYSELF?

This question can seem simple to answer, yet after kids it's common to feel lost and even confused about who you are now. Use the following statements to start to define how you see yourself.

- When those close to me describe me, they tend to highlight _____ about me.

- A quality I have that I'm really proud of is (list as many as you can) _____.
- When _____ happens and I respond by _____, I feel really distant from the person I think of myself as because I consider myself someone who is _____.
- Something about me that's really been challenged after becoming a mom is _____. I've realized that this is a part of me that (I need to change, I need to bring back, I need to be more flexible around).

## WHAT IS IMPORTANT TO ME?

The table on the next page gives some examples of things that you may say are important to you. First, start by checking which ones apply to you. Then try to order them from most important to least.

Now reflect on the following questions:

- What are the top five things that are important to me?
- What does living out each of these look like? Think through specific examples.
- What gets in the way of living these out?
- What changes can I make to maximize my top five most important items?

## WHAT BRINGS MY LIFE MEANING?

You can use the items you listed as most important to you to help you formulate what really brings your life meaning, or this may be something entirely different. There is no wrong answer here.

My life feels most meaningful to me when I (feel free to list as many as you want) . . .

| | | | |
|---|---|---|---|
| Family | Freedom | Security | Loyalty |
| Intelligence | Connection | Creativity | Humanity |
| Success | Respect | Invention | Diversity |
| Generosity | Integrity | Finesse | Love |
| Openness | Religion | Order | Advancement |
| Respect | Joy | Play | Forgiveness |
| Work Smarter and Harder | Excitement | Change | Goodness |
| Involvement | Faith | Wisdom | Beauty |
| Caring | Personal Development | Honesty | Adventure |
| Kindness | Teamwork | Career | Communication |
| Learning | Excellence | Innovation | Quality |
| Commonality | Contributing | Spirituality | Strength |
| Entertainment | Wealth | Speed | Power |
| Affection | Cooperation | Love of Career | Friendship/ Relationships |
| Encouragement | Pride in Your Work | Clarity | Charisma |
| Humor | Leadership | Renewal | Home |
| Authenticity | Contentment | Courage | Balance |
| Compassion | Fitness | Professionalism | Knowledge |
| Patience | Peace | Prosperity | Wellness |
| Finances | Gratitude | Grace | Endurance |
| Effectiveness | Fun | Fame | Justice |
| Appreciation | Willingness | Trusting Your Gut | Giving People a Chance |
| Harmony | Happiness | Self-Respect | Abundance |
| Reciprocity | Enjoyment | Entrepreneurship | Influence |

- When I'm creating something beautiful
- When I think about the impact I am having on my children
- When I am standing up for a cause I believe in
- When I am teaching people about something I'm passionate about
- When I connect with friends
- When I am earning a living for my family

## PUT IT ALL TOGETHER: ALIGNMENT

This is how I see my ideal self: _____.
This is how I view myself right now: _____.
One goal I can set to align more in this area is to _____.

(You can change your ideal to be more realistic or change to live up more to your ideal.)

| The top five things that are important to me are | I am living in alignment with this area (Y/N) |
| --- | --- |
|  |  |
|  |  |
|  |  |
|  |  |
|  |  |

What is one goal you can make to align what is important to you with how you're living your life?

The thing that brings my life the greatest meaning is _____.

One thing I can do to foster my ability to do more of what brings me meaning is _____.

## DEFINING YOUR ANCHOR

Use the list of things that are important to you and that bring you meaning to help inform your anchor. These can help to stir up thoughts.

Your anchor should be deeply meaningful to you. This isn't a mantra to just help mask difficult moments but rather something that tethers you to who you are and what is important to you.

When nothing is feeling right and the day is not going like you planned, if you are still tethered to your anchor, your day is still considered a success.

You can develop as many of these anchors as you need and even create new ones for different situations, inside or outside of motherhood moments. These may even change frequently throughout your day. For example, in my work life, I write out one important thing that I want to get done that day. If I complete that task, I consider the workday a success.

To come up with your anchor, try closing your eyes and imagining what success looks like to you in different moments. I'm not talking about conquering or dominating that particular moment but rather what is the stripped-down version of success.

Now, think of completing this sentence:

"If I _____, and nothing else, I will _____."

Here are some examples. But remember, your anchor should be meaningful to you, so don't just grab one from here unless it truly speaks to your heart.

- If I keep my cool, no matter what else happens, I'll consider it a success.
- If I fit in a moment for me, I will feel good about my day.
- If I conveyed my love to my kids today, I will release my guilt.
- If I had a moment of fun today with my kids, then it was a good day.
- If I used my gifts (insert here) today, I will consider the day productive.

Now you write yours: _____.

# REVIEWING THE FIVE STEPS
# OF THE RELATIONSHIP
# ATTACHMENT METHOD

**W**hat I hope you leave this book with is a clear plan for self-check-ins that you can easily access in moments when you feel disconnected from yourself. When you regularly make time to check in with you, you will never fully get lost in motherhood. You will have moments in which you are less recognizable, but you will have the know-how to quickly tune in to you and make the shifts you need in those moments. If you can't or don't have the time or energy to make the shifts at that very second, you will at least have definition to your experience. Definition offers comfort because it helps you relate to your circumstances differently. When you have definition, you are empowered to understand what's going on with you and even make a change rather than feeling disempowered by the overwhelming feeling of being lost and stuck.

Your plan is captured in a picture called the Relationship Attachment Model (RAM). The RAM is a picture of your relationship with yourself and is made up of five bonds (know, trust, rely, commit, and touch) that produce feelings of connection or disconnection. Each bond moves independently but has an impact on the overall arrangement of the bonds; when you move one down, the others may start to be pulled down over time. If you work on one area and it increases, the others will be affected and start to increase as well. The arrangement of the five bonds will tell you an overall story of the state of your relationship with yourself. This story will reflect how you feel in your relationship, and the arrangement of the five bonds will reveal the areas that need the most attention. This way you can be targeted with your care.

Here's the gist in bullet form for your quick review:

1. Each bond moves independently up and down and represents a range of closeness or distance in a relationship.
2. The bonds interact with one another. If one level is low, it can pull the others down. If a level is high, it can sometimes help move the other levels up.
3. The arrangement of the five bonds creates a pictorial representation of what is going on in the relationship and can quickly show vulnerabilities and targeted areas where you can make adjustments.

## YOUR PLAN FOR A SELF-CHECK-IN

When it is time for your self-check-in—and remember, once you've got this down, you can do this in the time it takes you to munch that chicken nugget from your kid's plate—the first thing you do is envision the picture of the RAM in your mind. This is your outline; everything flows from here.

Next, you adjust the levels in your mind to reflect how you are feeling in that moment. If you have more time and you want to journal it or draw it out, by all means do it, but know that it's not necessary.

When you have your picture and your levels are adjusted, you can tune in to one or more of the levels and ask yourself these questions.

KNOW DEEPLY: Who am I right now versus who I want to be?
TRUST ACCURATELY: What am I focusing on?
RELY BOLDLY: What do I need?
COMMIT WISELY: How am I prioritizing me versus all the other things?
TOUCH PURPOSEFULLY: What is my body saying to me?

These questions are shortcuts to the depth of content and tools I gave you in this book. They are your fast pass to figuring out what it is that you really need in that moment. Each of the five steps has ideal outcomes that you can begin to move toward little by little with each self-check-in or micro-adjustment along the way. I reviewed what these desired outcomes look like in the previous chapters, but so you have it all in one spot, here they are:

KNOW DEEPLY so that you can feel aligned with who you know yourself to be and so you can care for yourself in meaningful ways.
TRUST ACCURATELY so that you can see yourself in a positive light.
RELY BOLDLY so that you can assess, assert, and prioritize your needs.
COMMIT WISELY so that you prioritize yourself and all other things in ways that you are at peace with.
TOUCH PURPOSEFULLY so that you can listen to your body and care for it in impactful ways.

Once you have envisioned the RAM, adjusted the levels to match your current experience, and asked yourself these questions, you then decide how you want to take action.

Maybe you connect to something that anchors you to the person you want to be, maybe you shift your focus, maybe you do a quick in-the-moment reset, maybe you decide to assert a need that you've been suppressing, maybe you rearrange how you're prioritizing things in that moment, or maybe you tune in to your body and realize your stress is high and implement some strategies discussed in chapter 8.

Here's the thing. There is no right way. There is not a list of things you *must* do in order to care for you. There's not a formulaic approach that you have to follow. If this was entirely prescriptive, it would likely just become another area of life in which you'd feel like you're falling short or just another thing to do on your list. The goal is for you to tune in to you, for you to check in with you and determine what you need to feel more connected based on the capacity you have in that moment. Again, sometimes this means telling yourself, *Hey, you. I see you and what you need. I'll be with you soon.* And other times, you can make those adjustments immediately. But you are now equipped with a plan, and plans are powerful.

Simply put, you use the RAM to define what's going on with you and then you determine where and when you can realign.

Here are the steps for your self-check-in:

1. Define your current experience on the RAM (do it in your head or do it on paper). Move the levels up and down. If you need help, use these questions to guide you:

KNOW DEEPLY: Am I living in a way that is consistent with how I see myself?
TRUST ACCURATELY: Do I see myself in a positive light?
RELY BOLDLY: What do I need?
COMMIT WISELY: Am I a priority in my own life?
TOUCH PURPOSEFULLY: Am I caring for my physical body?

2.  Determine where, when, and how you will realign. If you need prompts to get you started, use these questions:

KNOW DEEPLY: Who am I right now versus who I want to be?

TRUST ACCURATELY: What am I focusing on?

RELY BOLDLY: What do I need?

COMMIT WISELY: How am I prioritizing me versus all the other things?

TOUCH PURPOSEFULLY: What is my body saying to me?

That's it. You can do it without anyone even knowing you're doing it. You can do it as you push a stroller, watch T-ball practice, roam the aisles of the grocery store, answer emails, give your kids a bath, drive to work, drink coffee in the morning, put on makeup, meditate, pray, or go for a walk. You can check in with you multiple times a day and make these micro-adjustments. And know this: there will be times when you will need to adjust something but you can't right then and there. For example, you may realize you've been bottling up your needs and you're ready to bring this up with your partner, but it isn't the right time. Or you may identify that you need to start a routine to care for your physical body, but you're not quite ready. You may have to put a pin in some of these things for now. But the helpful piece is that you have definition around what you need to do to care for you. You are now equipped with a plan.

# ACKNOWLEDGMENTS

I want to thank my husband, Chad, and two children, Effie and Roy. Bringing this book to life was a team effort. Supporting me through this process required sacrifice. You all took it in stride and were so affirming of how important this book was. Thank you for giving me time alone to get this done. Chad, thank you for your energy and time to make space for this in our lives. I appreciate you reading my chapters as I emerged from the basement office with a stack of papers in hand and reassuring me that "it's really good, babe." I love you and appreciate you so much.

Thank you to my father, John Van Epp. You are one of the best men I know. You're a brilliant mind and thinker. I've been blessed to have worked alongside you and learn from you for over fifteen years. Thank you for letting me use the RAM in my book. This is your baby, your legacy, and I know that I'm one of the only people on the planet you would grant this permission to. The magnitude of that gift will never be lost on me. You've empowered millions of lives with the RAM over your career, and I hope that I did it justice. I love you, Dad.

Thank you to my mom, Shirley Van Epp. You have given me the gift of a wonderful mother. Thank you for being my biggest cheerleader in life. Thank you for showing up with hot food and offering childcare when

I'm struggling. Thank you for your endless love, support, and generosity. I am so grateful for you. I love you, Mom.

Thank you to my sister, Jessica Berarducci. As I wrote this book, you were deep in the trenches raising littles and having babies. I had you top of mind often as I wrote these chapters, wondering *Would Jess find this helpful?* Sometimes I miss the ease of our carefree and kid-free times, laughing and chatting together. But it has been such a gift to watch you mother your children so graciously and gently. I love you.

Thank you to my mother- and father-in-law, Cindy and Larry Cutlip. You both have been so gracious in asking me questions about my book and expressive of how proud you are of me. I think you were the first to preorder my book when it appeared on Amazon. Thank you for your support and your son. I love you both.

Thank you to the McMahon family for your enthusiasm, connections, support, and friendship. Kelly, you offered me the most thoughtful edits throughout this process. You were always a yes when I texted, "Have a quick second for a book question?" Throughout our friendship, you've commented on how you think differently than most people; man, am I grateful that you do. Thank you for your beautiful mind and all the encouragement. Your friendship has been such a gift to me, and I will always be glad I awkwardly introduced myself to your babysitter, thinking there was hope of a mom friend next door.

Thank you to my friend Alex Glynn. I am blessed to have a friend who will travel into conversational depths that will make your head spin in the most fulfilling of ways. Your curiosity and genuine interest about life in general—and my book topic specifically—has been such a gift to me. Thank you for hopping on calls with me to obsess about the book title when you're running the show with three kids desperate for snacks. Thank you, my friend.

Thank you to my friend Lindsey Johnson. You are tough, so so talented, and such an impressive woman. I will never forget our walk around Dana Point Harbor where you told me, "Girl, you should just start an Instagram, just do it." I am grateful you pushed me to do something so far outside my comfort zone. Even though you live so far, I know that you are in my corner always, cheering me on. I appreciate you so much.

Thank you to Myla Leinweber. Our voice-memo conversations are often the highlight of my day. You help me feel less alone in a digital work-at-home world that can feel incredibly isolating. Thank you for your ideas, your energy, your enthusiasm, your questioning, your expertise, your Google Docs, and your generosity. You're such a kind and giving friend, I value you so much.

I want to thank Jazzmin Martinez. You are more than a sitter—you are part of our family. Thank you for loving our kids and caring for them so well when I needed help. Thank you for listening to me brainstorm content ideas endlessly, adding more to the conversation, and helping me on TikTok and with my Instagram stories. You dreamed one night about the phrase "Go Mom Yourself" and I'm forever grateful that you shared it with me. I appreciate you so much, thank you.

Thank you to Tracy Dalgleish. I've loved having a partner in this writing process. Being able to share our fears, frustrations, and ideas with each other has made this writing journey so much more manageable. We sure are doing a lot, my friend.

Thank you to Kait Tomlin. You didn't hesitate when I reached out to you to learn about your book-writing process and immediately connected me with your editor who was working as a literary agent. I am incredibly honored that you shared her information with me because the introduction to her changed the trajectory of my future. Thank you for trusting me with that relationship.

To my literary agent, Rachel Jacobson. You have felt like a friend through this process guiding me and offering thoughtful and honest feedback. Your ideas and editorial help putting together my proposal were invaluable. This process can be really overwhelming and downright confusing, and I am eternally grateful for your willingness to field my hundreds of Voxes. Thank you for your support and your encouragement and for believing in the message of this book and me. You are just the best.

# ACKNOWLEDGMENTS

Thank you to Rob Eager for encouraging me to drive the bus, when I was not sure of my place in all of this publishing business. Brigitta Nortker, thank you for your quiet and steady support. You are the fastest to respond to emails and offered the most thoughtful edits. And to the team at Nelson Books, I am grateful for your belief in me and your support throughout this process.

To my colleagues online: thank you. Specifically thank you to Bryce Reddy, Dr. Alice Pickering, Karrie Locher, Dr. Ashurina Ream, and Dr. Jazmin McCoy. You all gave me space on your accounts to conduct Q+A sessions when I was just getting started and I'm so thankful for your trust and allowing me that opportunity. Thank you to my colleagues for sharing about this book.

To my community on Instagram. What a wild world social media is; I am humbled and grateful for the women who entrust their precious time to me. Thank you for your support of this book; I hope it has helped you.

To God: I would be lost without your presence in my life. I know I'm fully loved and that is the ultimate gift.

# NOTES

## Chapter 1: We Mom So Hard

1. Harriet Lerner, *The Dance of Anger: A Woman's Guide to Changing the Patterns of Intimate Relationships* (New York: Harper & Row, 1985), 20.
2. Emily Nagoski and Amelia Nagoski, *Burnout: The Secret to Unlocking the Stress Cycle* (New York: Random House Publishing, 2020), xiii–ix.
3. Eve Rodsky, *Fair Play: A Game-Changing Solution for When You Have Too Much to Do (and More Life to Live)* (New York: Putnam, 2019), 7.
4. Susan J. Douglas and Meredith W. Michaels, *The Mommy Myth: The Idealization of Motherhood and How It Has Undermined Women* (New York: Free Press, 2004); Sharon Hays, *The Cultural Contradictions of Motherhood* (New Haven, CT: Yale University Press, 1996); Jodi Vandenberg-Daves, *Modern Motherhood: An American History* (New Brunswick, NJ: Rutgers University Press, 2014); Amy Westervelt, *Forget Having It All: How America Messed Up Motherhood and How to Fix It* (New York: Seal Press, 2018); Wendy Hollway, *Knowing Mothers: Researching Maternal Identity Change* (London: Palgrave Macmillan, 2015).
5. Sharon Hays, *The Cultural Contradictions of Motherhood* (New Haven, CT: Yale University Press, 1996), 6.
6. Pratyusha Tummala-Narra, "Contemporary Impingements on Mothering," *American Journal of Psychoanalysis* 69, no. 1 (March 2009): 4–21, https://doi.org/10.1057/ajp.2008.37; Jean-Anne Sutherland, "Mothering, Guilt and Shame," *Sociology Compass* 45, no. 5 (May 2010): 310–21, https://doi.org/10.1111/j.1751-9020.2010.00283.x; Ylva Elvin-Nowak, "Accompanied

by Guilt: Modern Motherhood the Swedish Way" (PhD diss., Stockholm University, 1999), http://su.diva-portal.org/smash/record.jsf?pid=diva2%3A456843&dswid=-7425.

7. Ruth Gaunt, "Maternal Gatekeeping: Antecedents and Consequences," *Journal of Family Issues* 29, no. 3 (March 2008): 373–95, https://doi.org/10.1177/0192513X07307851.

8. Holly H. Schiffrin, Kathryn Rizzo, and Miriam Liss, "Insight into the Parenthood Paradox: Mental Health Outcomes of Intensive Mothering," *Journal of Child and Family Studies* 22, no. 5 (June 2012): 614–20, https://psycnet.apa.org/doi/10.1007/s10826-012-9615-z.

9. Jean M. Twenge, W. Keith Campbell, and Craig A. Foster, "Parenthood and Marital Satisfaction: A Meta-Analytic Review," *Journal of Marriage and the Family* 65, no. 3 (August 2003): 574–83, https://www.jstor.org/stable/3600024; Esther S. Kluwer, "From Partnership to Parenthood: A Review of Marital Change Across the Transition to Parenthood," *Journal of Family Theory and Review* 2, no. 2 (June 2010): 105–25, https://doi.org/10.1111/j.1756-2589.2010.00045.x.

10. Douglas and Michaels, *Mommy Myth*, 6.

11. Suzanne M. Bianchi, John P. Robinson, and Melissa A. Milkie, *Changing Rhythms of American Family Life*, American Sociological Association's Rose Series in Sociology (New York: Russell Sage Foundation, 2006), 63–64.

12. "Motherhood Today: Tougher Challenges, Less Success," Pew Research Center, May 2, 2007, https://www.pewresearch.org/social-trends/2007/05/02/motherhood-today-tougher-challenges-less-success/.

13. Caroline Picard, "Gen Zers and Millennials Have Very Different Ideas of What It Means to Be the 'Perfect Parent,'" What to Expect, February 16, 2023, https://www.whattoexpect.com/news/first-year/gen-z-millennials-perfect-parent.

14. Christianna Silva, "The Millennial Obsession with Self-Care," Health: NPR, June 4, 2017, https://www.npr.org/2017/06/04/531051473/the-millennial-obsession-with-self-care.

15. "Parenting in America (2015 Survey Report)," Pew Research Center, December 17, 2015, https://www.pewresearch.org/social-trends/2015/12/17/parenting-in-america/.

16. "Parenting in America," Pew Research Center.

## Chapter 2: Mother Yourself Like You Mother Your Kids

1. "Motherly's 2020 State of Motherhood Survey Results," Motherly, May 6, 2020, https://www.mother.ly/news/state-of-motherhood-survey/.

2. Jessica Bennett et al., "The Primal Scream: America's Mothers Are in Crisis,"

*New York Times*, February 4, 2021, https://www.nytimes.com
/2021/02/04/parenting/working-moms-mental-health-coronavirus.html.

3. Emily Nagoski and Amelia Nagoski, *Burnout: The Secret to Unlocking the Stress Cycle* (New York: Ballantine Books, 2019), 8.

4. Radostina K. Purvanova and John P. Muros, "Gender Differences in Burnout: A Meta-Analysis," *Journal of Vocational Behavior* 77, no. 2 (October 2010): 168–85, https://doi.org/10.1016/j.jvb.2010.04.006.

5. D. W. Winnicott, *Playing and Reality* 2nd ed. (1971; repr., New York: Routledge Classics, 2005), 13.

6. Laura M. Padilla-Walker and Larry J. Nelson, "Black Hawk Down? Establishing Helicopter Parenting as a Distinct Construct from Other Forms of Parental Control During Emerging Adulthood," *Journal of Adolescence* 35, no. 5 (October 2012): 1177–90, https://doi.org/10.1016/j.adolescence.2012.03.007.

7. Holly H. Schiffrin et al., "Helping or Hovering? The Effects of Helicopter Parenting on College Students' Well-Being," *Journal of Child and Family Studies* 23, no. 3 (February 2013): 548–57, https://doi.org/10.1007/s10826-013-9716-3.

8. Suzanne Simard, *Intelligent Trees*, directed by Julia Dordel and Guido Tölke (Rhineland-Palatinate, Germany: Dorcon Film, 2016), streaming video, 45:00, https://www.amazon.com/Intelligent-Trees-Peter-Wohlleben/dp/B01LWIEY4F.

9. Simard, *Intelligent Trees*.

10. Akira Shimizu et al., "Fine-Tuned Bee-Flower Coevolutionary State Hidden Within Multiple Pollination Interactions," *Scientific Reports* 4 (February 2014), https://doi.org/10.1038/srep03988.

11. Abigail Tucker, *Mom Genes: Inside the New Science of Our Ancient Maternal Instinct* (New York: Gallery Books, 2021), 1.

12. Mads Kamper-Jorgensen et al., "Male Microchimerism and Survival Among Women," *International Journal of Epidemiology* 43, no. 1 (February 2014): 168–73, https://doi.org/10.1093/ije/dyt230.

## Chapter 4: Step 1: Know Deeply

1. Jean Laplanche and Jean-Bertrand Pontalis, "Compulsion to Repeat (Repetition Compulsion)," in *The Language of Psychoanalysis* (1967; repr., New York: Routledge, 2018), 19.

## Chapter 5: Step 2: Trust Accurately

1. Brené Brown, *Brené Brown: The Call to Courage*, directed by Sandra Restrepo (Los Angeles: Netflix, 2019), https://www.netflix.com/title/81010166.

2. Brian Tracy, "Focus Your Mind: Brian Tracy's Philosophy on Achieving Success," Law of Attraction, March 26, 2023, YouTube video, 13:05, https://www.youtube.com/watch?v=sTLvYVOvCVg.

3. Christopher Chabris and Daniel Simons, *The Invisible Gorilla: How Our Intuitions Deceive Us* (London: HarperCollins, 2011), 5–6.

4. Julie Bort, Aviva Pflock, and Devra Renner, *Mommy Guilt: Learn to Worry Less, Focus on What Matters Most, and Raise Happier Kids* (New York: Amacom, 2005), 4.

5. Please note: the exception to the quick-adjustment rule is that there may be seasons of life in which different expectations or impossible standards crop up. Remember long ago when I said that we have these dormant seeds that at different times of life provide the right conditions for growth? This is what I'm saying here. Becoming a mom may offer those conditions, school transitions may offer another, and an empty nest yet another. Keep this section handy to refer back to during major transitions so you can walk through this exercise again.

## Chapter 6: Step 3: Rely Boldly

1. John Bowlby, "The Nature of the Child's Tie to His Mother," *International Journal of Psychoanalysis* 39 no. 5 (September–October 1958): 350–73, https://pubmed.ncbi.nlm.nih.gov/13610508/.

2. Robbie Duschinsky, "Chapter 2: Mary Ainsworth and the Strange Situation Procedure," in *Cornerstones of Attachment Research* (Clarendon: Oxford University Press, 2020), 109–210, https://doi.org/10.1093/med-psych /9780198842064.003.0002.

3. Stan Tatkin, *Wired for Love: How Understanding Your Partner's Brain and Attachment Style Can Help You Diffuse Conflict and Build a Secure Relationship* (Oakland, CA: New Harbinger Publications, 2011); Amir Levine and Rachel S. F. Heller, *Attached: The New Science of Adult Attachment and How It Can Help You Find—and Keep—Love* (New York: TarcherPerigee, 2010).

4. Judith A. Crowell, Dominique Treboux, and Everett Waters, "Stability of Attachment Representations: The Transition to Marriage," *Developmental Psychology* 38, no.4 (2002): 467–79, https://doi.org/10.1037//0012 -1649.38.4.467; Diane Felmlee and Susan Sprecher, "Close Relationships and Social Psychology: Intersections and Future Paths," *Social Psychology Quarterly* 63, no. 4 (December 2000): 365–76, https://doi.org/10.2307 /2695846.

5. John W. Thibaut and Harold H. Kelley, *The Social Psychology of Groups* (New York: Routledge, 1959), https://doi.org/10.4324/9781315135007;

George Caspar Homans, *Social Behavior: Its Elementary Forms* (New York: Harcourt, Brace, and World, 1961); Peter M. Blau, "Justice in Social Exchange," *Sociological Inquiry* 34, no. 2 (April 1964): 193–206, http://dx.doi.org/10.1111/j.1475–682X.1964.tb00583.x.

## Chapter 7: Step 4: Commit Wisely

1. Roy F. Baumeister et al., "Ego Depletion: Is the Active Self a Limited Resource?," *Journal of Personality and Social Psychology* 74, no. 5 (1998): 1252–65, https://doi.org/10.1037/0022–3514.74.5.1252.
2. June J. Pilcher et al., "Interactions Between Sleep Habits and Self-Control," *Frontiers in Human Neuroscience* 9 (May 2015): 284, https://doi.org /10.3389/fnhum.2015.00284; Susan L. Worley, "The Extraordinary Importance of Sleep: The Detrimental Effects of Inadequate Sleep on Health and Public Safety Drive an Explosion of Sleep Research," *Pharmacy and Therapeutics* 43, no. 12 (December 2018): 758–63.
3. Sara W. Lazar et al., "Meditation Experience Is Associated with Increased Cortical Thickness," *Neuroreport* 16, no. 17 (November 2005): 1893–97.
4. Alison Reynard et al., "Heart Rate Variability as a Marker of Self-Regulation," *Applied Psychophysiology and Biofeedback* 36, no. 3 (July 2011): 209–15, https://doi.org/10.1007/s10484–011–9162–1.

## Chapter 8: Step 5: Touch Purposefully

1. Grace J. Chan et al., "What Is Kangaroo Mother Care? Systematic Review of the Literature," *Journal of Global Health* 6, no. 1 (June 2016): 1–9, https://doi.org/10.7189/jogh.06.010701.
2. Ann-Marie Widström et al., "Skin-to-Skin Contact the First Hours After Birth, Underlying Implications and Clinical Practice," *Acta Paediatrica* 108, no. 7 (July 2019): 1192–204, https://doi.org/10.1111/apa.14754.
3. Sanyukta Golaya, "Touch-Hunger: An Unexplored Consequence of the COVID-19 Pandemic," *Indian Journal of Psychological Medicine* 43, no. 4 (July 2021): 362–63, https://doi.org/10.1177/02537176211014469; Mariana von Mohr, Louise P. Kirsch, and Aikaterini Fotopoulou, "Social Touch Deprivation During COVID-19: Effects on Psychological Wellbeing and Craving Interpersonal Touch," *Royal Society Open Science* 8, no. 9 (September 2021), https://doi.org/10.1098/rsos.210287; Joanne Durkin, Debra Jackson, and Kim Usher, "Touch in Times of COVID-19: Touch Hunger Hurts," *Journal of Clinical Nursing* 30, no. 1–2 (January 2021): e4–e5, https://doi.org/10.1111/jocn.15488.
4. Harry F. Harlow, "The Nature of Love," *American Psychologist* 13, no. 12 (1958): 673–85, https://doi.org/10.1037/h0047884.

5. Jill Littrell, "The Mind-Body Connection: Not Just a Theory Anymore," *Social Work in Health Care* 46, no. 4 (November 2007): 17–37, https://doi.org/10.1300/J010v46n04_02.

6. Fariha Angum et al., "The Prevalence of Autoimmune Disorders in Women: A Narrative Review," *Cureus* 12 no. 5 (May 2020): e8094, https://doi.org/10.7759%2Fcureus.8094; Glinda S. Cooper and Berrit C. Stroehla, "The Epidemiology of Autoimmune Disease," *Autoimmunity Reviews* 2, no. 3 (May 2003): 119–25.

7. Ljudmila Stojanovich and Dragomir Marisavljevich, "Stress as a Trigger of Autoimmune Disease," *Autoimmunity Reviews* 7, no. 3 (January 2008): 209–13, https://doi.org/10.1016/j.autrev.2007.11.007.

8. Emily Nagoski and Amelia Nagoski, *Burnout: The Secret to Unlocking the Stress Cycle* (New York: Ballantine Books, 2019), 15.

9. Nagoski and Nagoski, *Burnout*, 21.

10. Eric Suni, "How Much Sleep Do We Really Need?," National Sleep Foundation, updated March 22, 2023, http://www.sleepfoundation.org/article/how-sleep-works/how-much-sleep-do-we-really-need.

11. Elizabeth Scott, "How to Relieve Stress with Art Therapy," Verywell Mind, January 24, 2020, https://www.verywellmind.com/art-therapy-relieve-stress-by-being-creative-3144581.

12. Kelly McGonigal, "How to Make Stress Your Friend," TED video, September 4, 2013, streaming video, 13:55, https://www.ted.com/talks/kelly_mcgonigal_how_to_make_stress_your_friend.

13. Abiola Keller et al., "Does the Perception That Stress Affects Health Matter? The Association with Health and Mortality," *Health Psychology* 31, no. 5 (September 2012): 677–84, https://doi.org/10.1037/a0026743.

14. Jenny J. W. Liu et al., "Re-conceptualizing Stress: Shifting Views on the Consequences of Stress and Its Effects on Stress Reactivity," *Plos One* 12, no. 3 (March 2017): e0173188, https://doi.org/10.1371/journal.pone.0173188.

15. "Never Alone but Always Lonely: The Social Isolation of Being a New Mother," Samuel Centre for Social Connectedness, March 8, 2019, https://www.socialconnectedness.org/never-alone-but-always-lonely-the-social-isolation-of-being-a-new-mother/.

16. Augustine Osei Boakye et al., "Juggling Between Work, Studies and Motherhood: The Role of Social Support Systems for the Attainment of Work–Life Balance," *SA Journal of Human Resource Management* 19 (October 2021): a1546, https://doi.org/10.4102/sajhrm.v19i0.1546; Pamela A. Andresen and Sharon L. Telleen, "The Relationship Between Social Support and Maternal Behaviors and Attitudes: A Meta-Analytic Review,

*American Journal of Community Psychology* 20, no. 6 (December1992): 753–74, https://doi.org/10.1007/BF00942236.

17. Elaine Aron, *The Highly Sensitive Person: How to Thrive When the World Overwhelms You* (New York: Citadel Press, 1996).

18. Maria Richter et al., "Do Words Hurt? Brain Activation During the Processing of Pain-Related Words," *Pain* 148, no. 2 (February 2010): 198–205, https://doi.org/10.1016/j.pain.2009.08.009.

19. Christopher Quinn-Nilas et al., "The Relationship Between Body Image and Domains of Sexual Functioning Among Heterosexual, Emerging Adult Women," *Sexual Medicine* 4, no. 3 (September 2016): e182–89, https://www.ncbi.nlm.nih.gov/pmc/articles/PMC5005305/.

# ABOUT THE AUTHOR

**D**r. Morgan Cutlip knows what it feels like to lose yourself in motherhood, and she's determined to help mothers navigate it better. Throughout her career, she has helped hundreds of thousands of people worldwide learn how to form and maintain healthy relationships. She is particularly experienced in translating psychological theory and research into practical, accessible, and actionable advice, which she shares with her clients and social media followers and through her blog, podcast, and courses on DrMorganCutlip.com. Dr. Morgan earned her master's in human development and family science and her doctorate in counseling psychology. She is a mother of two wild kids, wife of her high school sweetheart, and lifelong lover of all things relationships.